DATE DUE

11629

333.76
CHE

Cherrington, Mark.

Degradation of the
land.

MESA VERDE MIDDLE SCHOOL
POWAY UNIFIED SCHOOL DISTRICT

DEGRADATION OF THE LAND

EARTH • AT • RISK

EARTH • AT • RISK

DEGRADATION OF THE LAND

by Mark Cherrington

Introduction by
Russell E. Train

Chairman of
the Board of Directors,
World Wildlife Fund and
The Conservation Foundation

CHELSEA HOUSE PUBLISHERS

new york   philadelphia

CHELSEA HOUSE PUBLISHERS
EDITOR-IN-CHIEF: Remmel Nunn
MANAGING EDITOR: Karyn Gullen Browne
COPY CHIEF: Mark Rifkin
PICTURE EDITOR: Adrian G. Allen
ART DIRECTOR: Maria Epes
ASSISTANT ART DIRECTOR: Howard Brotman
MANUFACTURING DIRECTOR: Gerald Levine
SYSTEMS MANAGER: Lindsey Ottman
PRODUCTION MANAGER: Joseph Romano
PRODUCTION COORDINATOR: Marie Claire Cebrián

EARTH AT RISK
SENIOR EDITOR: Jake Goldberg

Staff for *Degradation of the Land*
ASSOCIATE EDITOR: Karen Hammonds
COPY EDITOR: Christopher Duffy
EDITORIAL ASSISTANT: Danielle Janusz
PICTURE RESEARCHER: Nisa Rauschenberg
SERIES DESIGNER: Maria Epes
SENIOR DESIGNER: Marjorie Zaum
COVER ILLUSTRATION: Bryn Barnard

First printing

1 3 5 7 9 8 6 4 2

Library of Congress Cataloging-in-Publication Data
Cherrington, Mark.
  Degradation of the land/by Mark Cherrington; introduction by
  Russell E. Train.
    p. cm.—(Earth at risk)
  Includes bibliographical references and index.
  Summary: Examines the problem of land degradation through
erosion and deforestation, discussing how these processes occur
and what effects they have.
  ISBN 0-7910-1589-0
      0-7910-1614-5 (pbk.)
  1. Soil degradation—Juvenile literature. 2. Soil
conservation—Juvenile literature. 3. Deforestation—Juvenile
literature. [1. Soil degradation. 2. Soil conservation.
3. Deforestation.]
I. Title. II. Series.   91-25517
S623.3.C47 1992   CIP
333.76′137—dc20   AC

C O N T E N T S

INTRODUCTION

Russell E. Train

Administrator, Environmental Protection Agency, 1973 to 1977; Chairman of the Board of Directors, World Wildlife Fund and The Conservation Foundation

There is a growing realization that human activities increasingly are threatening the health of the natural systems that make life possible on this planet. Humankind has the power to alter nature fundamentally, perhaps irreversibly.

This stark reality was dramatized in January 1989 when *Time* magazine named Earth the "Planet of the Year." In the same year, the Exxon *Valdez* disaster sparked public concern over the effects of human activity on vulnerable ecosystems when a thick blanket of crude oil coated the shores and wildlife of Prince William Sound in Alaska. And, no doubt, the 20th anniversary celebration of Earth Day in April 1990 renewed broad public interest in environmental issues still further. It is no accident then that many people are calling the years between 1990 and 2000 the "Decade of the Environment."

And this is not merely a case of media hype, for the 1990s will truly be a time when the people of the planet Earth learn the meaning of the phrase "everything is connected to everything else" in the natural and man-made systems that sustain our lives. This will be a period when more people will understand that burning a tree in Amazonia adversely affects the global atmosphere just as much as the exhaust from the cars that fill our streets and expressways.

Central to our understanding of environmental issues is the need to recognize the complexity of the problems we face and the relationships between environmental and other needs in our society. Global warming provides an instructive example. Controlling emissions of carbon dioxide, the principal greenhouse gas, will involve efforts to reduce the use of fossil fuels to generate electricity. Such a reduction will include energy conservation and the promotion of alternative energy sources, such as nuclear and solar power.

The automobile contributes significantly to the problem. We have the choice of switching to more energy efficient autos and, in the longer run, of choosing alternative automotive power systems and relying more on mass transit. This will require different patterns of land use and development, patterns that are less transportation and energy intensive.

In agriculture, rice paddies and cattle are major sources of greenhouse gases. Recent experiments suggest that universally used nitrogen fertilizers may inhibit the ability of natural soil organisms to take up methane, thus contributing tremendously to the atmospheric loading of that gas—one of the major culprits in the global warming scenario.

As one explores the various parameters of today's pressing environmental challenges, it is possible to identify some areas where we have made some progress. We have taken important steps to control gross pollution over the past two decades. What I find particularly encouraging is the growing environmental consciousness and activism by today's youth. In many communities across the country, young people are working together to take their environmental awareness out of the classroom and apply it to everyday problems. Successful recycling and tree-planting projects have been launched as a result of these budding environmentalists who have committed themselves to a cleaner environment. Citizen action, activated by youthful enthusiasm, was largely responsible for the fast-food industry's switch from rainforest to domestic beef, for pledges from important companies in the tuna industry to use fishing techniques that would not harm dolphins, and for the recent announcement by the McDonald's Corporation to phase out polystyrene "clam shell" hamburger containers.

Despite these successes, much remains to be done if we are to make ours a truly healthy environment. Even a short list of persistent issues includes problems such as acid rain, ground-level ozone and smog, and airborne toxins; groundwater protection and nonpoint sources of pollution, such as runoff from farms and city streets; wetlands protection; hazardous waste dumps; and solid waste disposal, waste minimization, and recycling.

Similarly, there is an unfinished agenda in the natural resources area: effective implementation of newly adopted management plans for national forests; strengthening the wildlife refuge system; national park management, including addressing the growing pressure of development on lands surrounding the parks; implementation of the Endangered Species Act; wildlife trade problems, such as that involving elephant ivory; and ensuring adequate sustained funding for these efforts at all levels of government. All of these issues are before us today; most will continue in one form or another through the year 2000.

Each of these challenges to environmental quality and our health requires a response that recognizes the complex nature of the problem. Narrowly conceived solutions will not achieve lasting results. Often it seems that when we grab hold of one part of the environmental balloon, an unsightly and threatening bulge appears somewhere else.

The higher environmental issues arise on the national agenda, the more important it is that we are armed with the best possible knowledge of the economic costs of undertaking particular environmental programs and the costs associated with not undertaking them. Our society is not blessed with unlimited resources, and tough choices are going to have to be made. These should be informed choices.

All too often, environmental objectives are seen as at cross-purposes with other considerations vital to our society. Thus, environmental protection is often viewed as being in conflict with economic growth, with energy needs, with agricultural productions, and so on. The time has come when environmental considerations must be fully integrated into every nation's priorities.

One area that merits full legislative attention is energy efficiency. The United States is one of the least energy efficient of all the industrialized nations. Japan, for example, uses far less energy per unit of gross national product than the United States does. Of course, a country as large as the United States requires large amounts of energy for transportation. However, there is still a substantial amount of excess energy used, and this excess constitutes waste. More fuel efficient autos and home heating systems would save millions of barrels of oil, or their equivalent, each year. And air pollutants, including greenhouse gases, could be significantly reduced by increased efficiency in industry.

I suspect that the environmental problem that comes closest to home for most of us is the problem of what to do with trash. All over the world, communities are wrestling with the problem of waste disposal. Landfill sites are rapidly filling to capacity. No one wants a trash and garbage dump near home. As William Ruckelshaus, former EPA administrator and now in the waste management business, puts it, "Everyone wants you to pick up the garbage and no one wants you to put it down!"

At the present time, solid waste programs emphasize the regulation of disposal, setting standards for landfills, and so forth. In the decade ahead, we must shift our emphasis from regulating waste disposal to an overall reduction in its volume. We must look at the entire waste stream, including product design and packaging. We must avoid creating waste in the first place. To the greatest extent possible, we should then recycle any waste that is produced. I believe that, while most of us enjoy our comfortable way of life and have no desire to change things, we also know in our hearts that our "disposable society" has allowed us to become pretty soft.

Land use is another domestic issue that might well attract legislative attention by the year 2000. All across the United States, communities are grappling with the problem of growth. All too often, growth imposes high costs on the environment—the pollution of aquifers; the destruction of wetlands; the crowding of shorelines; the loss of wildlife habitat; and the loss of those special places, such as a historic structure or area, that give a community a sense of identity. It is worth noting that growth is not only the product of economic development but of population movement. By the year 2010, for example, experts predict that 75% of all Americans will live within 50 miles of a coast.

It is important to keep in mind that we are all made vulnerable by environmental problems that cross international borders. Of course, the most critical global conservation problems are the destruction of tropical forests and the consequent loss of their biological capital. Some scientists have calculated extinction rates as high as 11 species per hour. All agree that the loss of species has never been greater than at the present time; not even the disappearance of the dinosaurs can compare to today's rate of extinction.

In addition to species extinctions, the loss of tropical forests may represent as much as 20% of the total carbon dioxide loadings to the atmosphere. Clearly, any international approach to the problem of global warming must include major efforts to stop the destruction of forests and to manage those that remain on a renewable basis. Debt for nature swaps, which the World Wildlife Fund has pioneered in Costa Rica, Ecuador, Madagascar, and the Philippines, provide a useful mechanism for promoting such conservation objectives.

Global environmental issues inevitably will become the principal focus in international relations. But the single overriding issue facing the world community today is how to achieve a sustainable balance between growing human populations and the earth's natural systems. If you travel as frequently as I do in the developing countries of Latin America, Africa, and Asia, it is hard to escape the reality that expanding human populations are seriously weakening the earth's resource base. Rampant deforestation, eroding soils, spreading deserts, loss of biological diversity, the destruction of fisheries, and polluted and degraded urban environments threaten to spread environmental impoverishment, particularly in the tropics, where human population growth is greatest.

It is important to recognize that environmental degradation and human poverty are closely linked. Impoverished people desperate for land on which to grow crops or graze cattle are destroying forests and overgrazing even more marginal land. These people become trapped in a vicious downward spiral. They have little choice but to continue to overexploit the weakened resources available to them. Continued abuse of these lands only diminishes their productivity. Throughout the developing world, alarming amounts of land rendered useless by over-grazing and poor agricultural practices have become virtual wastelands, yet human numbers continue to multiply in these areas.

From Bangladesh to Haiti, we are confronted with an increasing number of ecological basket cases. In the Philippines, a traditional focus of U.S. interest, environmental devastation is widespread as defores-tation, soil erosion, and the destruction of coral reefs and fisheries combine with the highest population growth rate in Southeast Asia.

Controlling human population growth is the key factor in the environmental equation. World population is expected to at least double to about 11 billion before leveling off. Most of this growth will occur in the poorest nations of the developing world. I would hope that the United States will once again become a strong advocate of international efforts to promote family planning. Bringing human populations into a sustainable balance with their natural resource base must be a vital objective of U.S. foreign policy.

Foreign economic assistance, the program of the Agency for International Development (AID), can become a potentially powerful tool for arresting environmental deterioration in developing countries. People who profess to care about global environmental problems— the loss of biological diversity, the destruction of tropical forests, the greenhouse effect, the impoverishment of the marine environment, and so on—should be strong supporters of foreign aid planning and the principles of sustainable development urged by the World Commission on Environment and Development, the "Brundtland Commission."

If sustainability is to be the underlying element of overseas assistance programs, so too must it be a guiding principle in people's practices at home. Too often we think of sustainable development only in terms of the resources of other countries. We have much that we can and should be doing to promote long-term sustainability in our own resource management. The conflict over our own rainforests, the old growth forests of the Pacific Northwest, illustrates this point.

The decade ahead will be a time of great activity on the environmental front, both globally and domestically. I sincerely believe we will be tested as we have been only in times of war and during the Great Depression. We must set goals for the year 2000 that will challenge both the American people and the world community.

Despite the complexities ahead, I remain an optimist. I am confident that if we collectively commit ourselves to a clean, healthy environment we can surpass the achievements of the 1980s and meet the serious challenges that face us in the coming decades. I hope that today's students will recognize their significant role in and responsibility for bringing about change and will rise to the occasion to improve the quality of our global environment.

The earth's fertile soils can support a tremendous amount of life, but human activity is taking an increasing toll on these ecosystems.

chapter 1

THE FOUNDATION
OF LIFE

If there is one resource on the earth that its inhabitants most take for granted, it is probably dirt: not the grime that collects on closet floors but the soil beneath people's feet. It seems so fundamental, so abundant, that it is hardly given a thought. Soil serves as the foundation for buildings and gives plants a place to take root. When it rains excessively, soil can turn to mud and call attention to itself by making travel difficult, but beyond that, it receives little notice. It is considered inert raw material, useful in its way, but environmentally, hardly cause for concern in the way that, for example, endangered species are. When a bulldozer plows up a scoop full of earth and dumps it unceremoniously in a heap to the side of a building project, no one jumps to protect it as they would a condor or a seal. Yet in the end, the degradation of the land may prove to be the most critical environmental concern of all.

Soil is the foundation of life on this planet. Plants, including the food crops upon which humankind depends, must have healthy soil in which to grow, and every other form of life depends ultimately on plants. The soil also serves as a storage tank and filter for the world's water, and healthy soil and healthy plant cover play an important role in determining the earth's climate. Damaging the soil is somewhat like pulling the bottom card out of a house of cards: The rest of the structure cannot remain standing. Over the past hundred years or so, humans have been pulling cards out from under themselves—by chopping down forests, draining swamps, watering deserts, planting foreign crops, removing protective plant cover, damming rivers, and pumping farmlands full of deadly chemicals.

Each year, humans cut down approximately 40 million acres of forests. They add nearly 300 billion pounds of fertilizers and more than 6 billion pounds of toxic pesticides to the soil. More than 24 billion tons of irreplaceable topsoil is lost annually, and 80,000 square miles of the planet's surface is turned into desert. This destruction is occurring in both industrialized and developing nations, from the United States to Latin America to the People's Republic of China. This widespread land degradation represents a potential threat to human survival. To understand why this is so, one must first understand the properties of soil.

THE SOIL

Soil comes in an enormous variety of textures, colors, and qualities. Most everyone is familiar with two common soil components: sand and clay. Both are made up of particles of rock minerals, clay being finer-grained than sand. A mineral substance with a consistency between these two materials is silt. Another important soil ingredient is humus, or decomposing plant and animal matter. Different mixtures of these and other sub-stances—including coarser rock called gravel, air, water, and various living organisms—create different types of soil at different depths in the earth.

Mature soils contain distinct layers called *soil horizons*. The surface layer of soil is called the topsoil, or *A-horizon*. This section holds most of the nutrients, living organisms, and organic matter (decaying plants and animals) and is generally darker and looser than the layers beneath it. Topsoil usually reaches a depth of about one foot but may extend to depths of three to four feet.

Below this very active organic layer lies what soil scientists, or *agronomists*, refer to as the *B-horizon*. It contains a mixture of organic and inorganic matter. Chemicals and minerals that are washed through the topsoil—a process called *leaching*— end up in the B-horizon. Fine-grained clay particles that are washed down to this layer render it denser than the topsoil. Below the B-horizon is the *C-horizon*, composed mostly of partially weathered rock. And beneath it lies the *bedrock*, the solid subsurface rock from which the finer rock particles in the soil above are derived.

Soil formation begins when surface rock or bedrock is exposed to the elements, such as rain or wind, in physical and chemical processes called *weathering*. Falling rainwater can loosen particles of surface rock. Water that percolates through the soil can further weaken and break up rock if it freezes. Water expands when it freezes. (That is why ice-cube trays only partly filled with water become fully filled with the frozen cubes.) If water happens to be in a crack in a rock when it freezes, the force of its expansion can be great enough to actually split the rock in two.

Chemicals of various kinds—such as acids and salts—are often contained in rainwater, and these, too, help disintegrate

rock. Sand carried by winds can also break up rock, as can
the growing roots of plants. As these processes occur over and
over, what was once bedrock gradually breaks down into finer
particles. But soil is much more than simply ground-up stone.
As various kinds of rock mix together, they interact chemically,
creating electric charges and determining the soil's acidity or
alkalinity, chemical properties that affect the soil's ability to
sustain various life-forms.

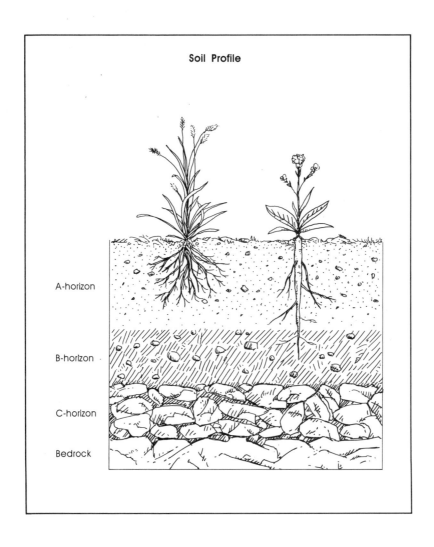

Soil Profile

A-horizon

B-horizon

C-horizon

Bedrock

Soil's color and texture vary depending on its chemical composition and the relative amounts of clay, sand, silt, gravel, and organic matter. The clay that is present to some degree in every kind of soil helps bind coarser particles together in small clumps. Gaps—or pores—between clumps allow water and gases including air, to permeate the earth. The number of pores in a given volume of soil and the distance between them determine the soil's *porosity*. Highly porous soils hold more water and air than those with low porosity.

Another soil characteristic is its *permeability*, the capacity of the soil to allow air and water to move through it. The best type of soil for growing most crops, called *loam*, contains a crumbly mixture of sand, silt, and clay that can absorb a lot of water but is highly permeable.

Another important component of soil is the large number of animals, plants, and microorganisms that live in it and contribute a variety of nutrients to its makeup. A handful of the most inert-looking soil is actually teeming with billions of tiny worms, filaments of fungus, spores, bits of decaying leaves, animal droppings, rotting wood, and bacteria. Harvard biologist E. O. Wilson estimates that a cubic inch of typical soil in the northeastern United States contains 5,000 different species of microorganisms.

Soil is never exactly the same in any two places, and in any given place, it changes over time, even from one day to the next. Soils in different locations vary depending on the different kinds of parent rock from which they are formed. They can also be changed by foreign sediments added by floodwaters, winds, volcanic eruptions, or inundation by oceans. Various climates dictate different kinds of plants and animals and different microorganisms, again changing the nature of the soil.

The U.S. Department of Agriculture classifies soils into 10 major types depending on their state of development, as evidenced by their color, texture, acidity, and the other factors discussed above. These so-called soil orders include semiarid grassland soils, called *mollisols*, with thick fertile topsoil suitable for crops; moderately fertile deciduous forest *alfisols*; light-colored desert *aridisols*, which are dry and tend to be infertile; and tropical rainforest *oxisols* with thin, easily damaged topsoil. As later chapters will illustrate, the physical and chemical properties of the soil determine what can and cannot be grown in a given place and play major roles in land degradation.

All soils are in a continual state of flux—some more than others. Soil components are added by rainfall, animal activity, and decaying vegetation, and they are removed by plants and animals that use them as nutrients, as well as by water, which washes them down through the soil and out to rivers and streams. The ingredients of soil are heated by the sun and frozen by the cold of winter and the chill of night. They are compacted by passing animals and vehicles and torn up by pig snouts, bull-dozers, and tree roots. The soil, then, is not so much a specific, static substance as a kind of *ecosystem*, a community of inter-acting, interdependent organisms and elements, which includes the plants and animals that grow in it. If any of these organisms or elements—plants, rocks, chemicals, water, sunlight, or micro-organisms—are changed, the whole system is affected.

Humankind is now greatly altering the earth's fragile soil ecosystems. People have found ways to boost farm production; to obtain more from the land through fertilizers, industrial farming, slash-and-burn forest clearing, and irrigation; and to move onto lands that never before supported them. But these accomplishments are short-lived, exploiting the bounty of eons of geological and biological development. To use an economic analogy, the planetary ecosystem functions on regular income—the day-to-day transfer of nutrients, water, and air—as well as savings. The savings take such forms as extra depth in the topsoil and underground reservoirs of water. Human productivity can appear to be greater than the natural system's because it draws not only on the regular income but also on the savings. If the reservoirs are used up and the topsoil is destroyed, there will be no resources left, and the natural system may not be able to revive itself.

There may be time, however, to preserve or rescue much of the earth's valuable land, provided enough people acquire an understanding of the nature of the problem and a commitment to solving it. This book will describe the various sources and types of land degradation as well as efforts underway around the world to halt this destruction. As the world becomes ever more industrialized and crowded, the stress on the land will grow—as will the challenge to save it.

Soils are affected by weather, plants, and the activities of creatures that eat, sleep, and move about on them.

An Idaho farmer readies his field for corn planting. Modern agricultural practices ease the task of cultivation but can have adverse long-term effects on the soil.

A G R I C U L T U R A L   C R I S I S

The popular image of farmers is of people living quiet lives in harmony with the land, coaxing from it the food needed by humankind in order to live. What could be more beneficial or more environmentally wholesome? Certainly, farms or ranches are not thought of as environmental hazards in the same way as are factories or refineries. In fact, farmers and ranchers, however well-intentioned, do considerable damage to the earth. In 1991, they will render more than 100,000 square miles of land sterile, poison more than a million people, and disrupt the delicate natural systems of countless acres of valuable soil.

It is important to understand that farmers do not cause this destruction deliberately. Often they are unaware of the problems they create, and even when they are aware, they cannot easily stop. The farming techniques that cause the damage also produce the larger harvests farmers now generally need to make a living and upon which the burgeoning human population depends. Yet the destruction of fertile land is clearly not in the long-term interests of either farmers or consumers.

To understand the impact of agriculture on the land, it helps to understand the role of plants in soil ecosystems. The roots of plants break up rock and keep soil from getting too compact while at the same time promoting an exchange of gases, nutrients, chemicals, and liquids. Roots also hold the soil together, preventing erosion. These actions occur on a scale that is hard to imagine just by looking at plants at the earth's surface. An average rye plant, for example, has 14 billion root hairs that, if placed end to end, would stretch 6,000 miles. Altogether, these root hairs grow 100 miles a day and have a total absorbing surface area larger than 10 football fields. And this is only one plant—an acre of rye might contain tens of thousands of plants, each with the same extensive root system. Other plant species also have extensive root systems and have a large impact on the soil.

Properly grown in appropriate soil, crops can benefit the land; improperly cultivated, they can destroy it. Modern farming methods, which emphasize the use of machinery, chemicals, and irrigation, can impoverish the soil and disrupt the environment, especially if they are employed on marginal lands. The same is true for ranching, which can deteriorate the land in a number of ways, especially where large numbers of livestock lead to overgrazing.

THE FARM AS FACTORY

Today less than 2% of the population produces all of the food grown in the United States. This was not always the case, however. At the beginning of the 20th century, more than half of the U.S. population was involved in agricultural production, mostly on small, family-owned farms. The work was carried out for the most part by horses, mules, and humans. Motorized farm machinery was rare and inefficient, and harvests were much smaller than they are today.

This system began to change in the early 20th century. As more and more people moved from the country to higher-paying jobs in the city, fewer farmers were left to produce greater and greater amounts of food to feed the growing population. This dilemma coincided with the development of more efficient internal combustion engines, which soon found their way into tractors, trucks, and harvesters. This new machinery allowed a single farmer to plant and harvest more crops, but even so, growers could barely keep up with the increasing demand for food.

It was not long before farmers realized that they could apply to crops the same kinds of production-line methods that

Before the advent of tractors and other machinery, most farmers relied on horses to plow land and harvest their crops.

factories were using. In other words, if they planted larger areas of land with a *monoculture,* or just one crop, season after season, they could buy their seed and supplies in bulk to save money. They could also streamline their planting and harvesting and focus all their energies on just one farming technique. From a business standpoint, this idea worked beautifully. Farmers were able to increase their yields and their profits tremendously.

This new practice also proved beneficial, however, for various crop-eating insects. If any of their preferred crops were planted, they were provided with a feast that stretched from horizon to horizon. If, for example, a farmer planted his field in wheat, it was bad news for insects that did not eat wheat, but the ones that did soon had booming populations. The same was true for wild plants that grew well in the vicinity of a particular crop. These weeds flourished where monocultures were implemented. But once again, technology provided a solution to the problem: *pesticides.* By spraying newly developed poisonous chemicals on crops, farmers could virtually eliminate insect pests and weeds with very little work. Also, starting in the 1940s, chemical companies began producing *fertilizers* that could boost the fertility of flagging soils overnight. Their development initially proved a boon to farmers and led to even greater harvests—the modern industrial farm was born.

Farming was also revolutionized by the development of *hybrid* crops, new plants created by the crossbreeding of existing species. The goal of this plant breeding was to combine the best traits of different species to produce crops with higher yields, resistance to diseases, and other desirable characteristics. Similar advances were made in livestock breeding, producing such

Plant breeders in China have developed a higher-yielding, disease-resistant variety of jute, a plant used to make sacking and twine.

animals as American Brahman cattle, which could flourish in hot climates such as that in the western United States.

By the 1960s, these various new techniques and products were so effective that industrialized nations began exporting them to developing countries in what became known as the Green Revolution. Soon most of the world was using monocropping, farm machinery, pesticides, and new strains of plants to produce bumper crops. It seemed a miracle. Hunger, it appeared, would be eliminated, and people would be freed to pursue other, less demanding ways of life.

But underneath all of the profit and promise, enormous problems lurked. The tractors and trucks that let a single man do the work of a hundred also compacted the soil as they moved, squashing the vital passages for air and water. The microorganisms and plant roots that needed that air and water began to die, leaving the soil weak. And the now-hardened and compacted earth, stripped of all vegetation except the crop plants, could no longer absorb water the way it once had. When rain fell, it would simply run off the surface into ditches, carrying with it tons of precious topsoil.

The idea of monoculture farming, which worked so well from a business standpoint, was an environmental disaster. In ecological terms, variety equals stability. The more varieties of plants that grow in a particular piece of soil, the more resilience that soil has. More nutrients are added to the soil from more sources, there are more outlets for the exchange of chemicals and gases, and the soil is healthier as a result. Where there is only one kind of crop, there will be only one source of nutrients, chemicals, and gases, and always the same ones. Furthermore, the crop quickly depletes all the nutrients in the soil that are useful to it. Bacteria and microorganisms that interact with that particular crop prosper, but all the thousands of others disappear. The soil soon becomes like a person who eats nothing but hamburgers: undernourished and weak. There is no easy way to measure this kind of soil nutrient depletion other than in falling crop yields, and in most cases, smaller yields are avoided by the application of fertilizers.

FERTILIZERS

Just as taking vitamins helps the hamburger eater, fertilizers can invigorate worn-out soil, but there is a price to be paid. Farmers used to fertilize land primarily with animal dung, either from cattle and horses or from seabird and bat droppings. Such natural fertilizers have been used for centuries, and in modest quantities, they work fairly well and with few side effects. But modern farming relies on synthetic chemical fertilizers to do the same job, and many of these, such as nitrate and phosphate compounds, are toxic to humans if they are ingested in large enough quantities.

Furthermore, unlike natural fertilizers, chemical products do not add much-needed humus to the soil. Eventually, the worn-out, compacted earth can no longer hold and absorb water as it used to, making it more difficult to farm. Any rain that makes it past the surface passes right through the soil unabsorbed. It also carries with it any chemicals, including fertilizers, that happen to be there. The water then works its way into underground water sources, and the chemicals travel into lakes, streams, and public drinking water supplies.

Today farmers worldwide put an average of 90 pounds of fertilizer on every acre of land, with the greatest concentrations (between 200 and 500 pounds per acre) in Europe, the Middle East, and Japan, followed closely by the United States, Asia, and Australia, which each use between 50 and 200 pounds per acre. By any reckoning, that is a lot of fertilizer, and massive amounts are finding their way into drinking water. Almost 2 million people in England drink water containing levels of nitrates above the allowable safety limits. And recently, one-fifth of all wells tested in the United States by the Environmental Protection Agency had unnaturally high levels of nitrates.

Fertilizers cause other problems as well. Because they are designed to enhance plant growth, that is just what they do when they get into ponds and rivers, causing what is called *eutrophication.* The green algae that are found naturally on pond, lake, and ocean surfaces get a huge boost from the draining fertilizer, and *algal blooms* soon thickly cover the water surface, cutting off light and absorbing the oxygen in the water, making it uninhabitable for fish and other plants and animals. In one extreme case in 1988, an algal bloom off the Scandinavian coast killed millions of fish and severely damaged the region's fishing industry. In the United States, Chesapeake Bay in Maryland is one of the best-known victims of this problem.

PESTICIDES

As deadly as fertilizers can be, pesticides are far worse. These chemicals are designed specifically to be toxic, and billions of pounds of them are sprayed on plants every year: *herbicides* to kill unwanted plants, *insecticides* to destroy insects and other organisms that might harm crops. As is the case with fertilizers,

Armed with a protective mask and rubber gloves, a farmer sprays fruit trees with pesticides. These chemicals protect crops from insects and other pests but can contaminate the environment and poison farmers and consumers.

water washing through damaged soil carries the chemicals into underground water supplies and so eventually to humans. In addition, the pesticides end up on the fruits, vegetables, and grains themselves and so can be eaten directly.

Between contaminated water and food and direct exposure to pesticides during spraying, more than 2 million people suffer acute pesticide poisoning each year worldwide, and as many as 40,000 die, according to the Worldwatch Institute. The U.S. National Academy of Sciences estimates that 20,000 people die each year in the United States from cancers caused by pesticide-contaminated water and food.

Pesticides do not kill just people. An insect that has eaten pesticide-treated plants and carries the poisonous chemicals in its body may be eaten by some other animal. That second animal may eat hundreds of insects, accumulating more and more toxin in its body. That animal and others like it may in turn be eaten by a larger predator. The larger the predator and the higher up it is on the so-called *food chain*, the greater are its chances of consuming dangerous quantities of pesticides. The most famous example of this phenomenon was the near-extinction of two top predators, the bald eagle and the peregrine falcon, from poisoning by the pesticide DDT.

Ironically, pesticides, for all their danger to people, are becoming less and less deadly to insects. Through a process called evolution, insects can develop immunities to chemical toxins; these were a primary defensive tool of the plants on which insects feed long before farmers began applying manufactured pesticides. These immunities develop through mutations, or changes in the organisms' genes—cellular material that transmits hereditary characteristics from one generation to another.

Predators such as ospreys that are high up on the food chain can accumulate dangerous, sometimes fatal quantities of pesticides in their body.

Through the combination of very short generations and extraordinary genetic flexibility, insect species frequently evolve a resistance to a new chemical within a few decades.

To make matters worse, insects can develop a resistance not only to a specific chemical but to all chemicals in the same family, so that it may take only a few years to evolve a resistance to a new but related pesticide. The end result is that there are now more than 400 species of arthropods (insects, ticks, and mites) as well as many bacteria and viruses that are immune to one or more of the pesticides used against them. This development is not only bothersome but dangerous, because frustrated farmers tend to apply more and more of the pesticides when they fail, thus increasing the danger to humans and animals. This is particularly common in the Third World, where farmers are often not fully aware of the hazards of the chemicals they are using. In addition, certain dangerous pesticides, such as DDT, that are banned in the United States and other industrialized nations are still widely used in developing countries.

An additional drawback to both fertilizers and pesticides, and to mechanized farming in general, is the immense amount of energy—mostly petroleum products—required to operate the tractors and other farm machinery that plow, sow seeds, distribute fertilizer and pesticides, and harvest crops. Petroleum derivatives are also used to manufacture many of the fertilizers and pesticides themselves. Agricultural production in the United States is especially energy-intensive. Each acre of U.S. cropland requires an energy input equal to about 150 gallons of oil, according to ecologist David Pimentel of Cornell University.

Crop dusting, in which pesticides are sprayed on plants from an airplane, is a common practice but an inefficient one. No more than 10% of the chemicals sprayed reach their intended targets.

Other Western nations also have energy-intensive farming practices, and energy use in Third World agriculture is rising fast. This intensive oil consumption adds to both the cost of farming and to the drain on the world's energy supplies.

LIVESTOCK FARMING

Livestock and poultry farming also contribute significantly to land degradation. Currently, more than twice as many rangeland and farm animals inhabit the earth than do humans, including more than 3 billion cattle, sheep, and goats and more than 9 billion chickens and other domestic fowl—and this population is growing.

Livestock production causes land degradation in a number of ways, both directly and indirectly. Inappropriate techniques can cause overgrazing of rangelands, destroying grasses and making the soil vulnerable to erosion. Additionally, intensive livestock production, in which animals are grain-fed rather than ranged, has some of the same drawbacks as modern "factory farming." Large quantities of chemical fertilizers and pesticides are often used, as are huge amounts of water and energy. Producing a pound of beef requires 20 to 40 times more energy than is needed to produce an amount of grain or beans with the same caloric value, according to David Pimentel.

Increasing livestock populations and the deterioration of existing grazing lands also lead to forest clearing to create more grazing land—often in regions unsuitable for this type of farming. Ranchers and herders are also moving onto marginal lands that are easily damaged and can even be turned into desert. (The

Beef cattle graze on an Oregon farm. Overgrazing of livestock can damage rangelands, causing soil erosion and other environmental problems.

consequences of livestock farming are discussed in more detail in chapters 5 and 6.)

SOLUTIONS

Solving the problems created by modern agricultural methods is not easy. If farmers simply stopped using fertilizers and pesticides, their crops—the world's food supply—would be cut in half. And if they stopped using machines, the drop would be even greater. If farmers are to wean themselves from chemicals and machinery, they need to do it gradually. In addition, modern farming in most developed countries is heavily tied to complex regulations and government subsidies.

Agricultural reform can also be hindered by economic factors that are often beyond the control of the farmers themselves. Many developing countries, for example, are deep in debt—to the tune of more than $1.3 trillion—to industrialized nations. The governments of the indebted nations encourage the growing of huge quantities of *cash crops,* those that can be sold to foreigners to raise money to repay debts. Such intensive farming-for-export can severely strain both cropland and rangeland but is hard to stop—environmentally responsible farming methods tend to take a backseat to economic crises.

Nonetheless, there are a number of potentially profitable strategies—some old, some new—that hold promise for ending destructive agricultural practices. Some of these are already in use. One widespread soil conservation practice that maintains soil fertility and reduces erosion, or topsoil loss, is *crop rotation.* This practice involves planting nutrient-depleting crops such as corn and cotton one year, and nutrient-restoring, ground-covering crops such as legumes (e.g., peas, beans, and alfalfa), or cereal plants such as oats, the next.

Soil that is highly erodible or infertile must be cultivated with particular care. The U.S. Department of Agriculture Soil Conservation Service has developed a land capability classification system that categorizes land into one of eight classes depending on the slope, soil quality, and drainage ability. It recommends varying conservation measures for each class. For some types of land the agency recommends that no farming take place whatsoever.

Many soil conservationists currently advocate the practice of what is called *low-input agriculture,* or farming that seeks to produce high yields using as few fertilizers, pesticides, fossil fuels, and other inputs as possible. Another goal of this method is maintaining farmland's long-term productivity—in other words, using it sustainably. In 1987, the U.S. Department of Agriculture began operating a Low-Input/Sustainable Agriculture (LISA) program that assists farmers in implementing low-input farming methods. Early results from the program indicate that low-input farming can often be profitable: The lower crop yields grown using this approach are offset by lower costs, enabling farmers to make a profit.

An approach that is related to low-input farming is *organic farming*, or cultivation using few or no chemicals. Organic farmers use natural fertilizers, such as crop waste and animal manure, that restore nutrients to soil and improve its structure, unlike chemical fertilizers. Organic farmers also incorporate *integrated pest management* (IPM) methods, which reduce pest damage by natural means rather than by using pesticides. One tactic is to introduce natural pest predators, or animals that eat insect pests. Pest predators have been used successfully in Africa and in the United States. Another pest-control technique, developed by Miami University researcher Gary Barrett, involves planting narrow strips of wild plants between crop fields. The strips of wild plants reduce the problems caused by the monocrop fields, serving as windbreaks, water regulators, and wildlife habitats. Pests are stopped by the natural barriers, which they cannot eat, and pest predators can live in the barriers, helping to control pest numbers. Preliminary results suggest this technique may be almost as effective as chemical pesticides in controlling insect damage.

Like low-input agriculture, organic farming tends to produce smaller yields but at lower cost; thus this type of farming can be profitable. In a study by ecologist Barry Commoner, yields of organic farmers averaged 11% less than those produced using conventional methods, but the net income per acre was almost

Strips of wild grasses grown between crop fields help restore nutrients to the soil and prevent erosion.

the same because of lower production costs. The organic farmers studied used 60% less fossil fuel, for example. So far, however, organic farming has proved difficult to practice on large-scale, industrial farms.

One of the most interesting and radical farming methods now drawing attention comes from an unlikely source: the field of archaeology. A British archaeologist named Peter Reynolds has studied the farming techniques of Iron Age farmers who developed metalwork in Britain about 2,500 years ago. Through his excavations and modern re-creations of their gardens, he has found that these farmers developed techniques that actually made the soil richer with each year that it was farmed. The key to their success was the use of plants native to the area, planted in as great a variety as possible in any given plot—a practice known as *intercropping*. Moreover, these ancient farmers did not weed or water their gardens, probably reasoning that all the plants, including what would now be called weeds, helped the soil-plant system function.

When Reynolds re-created one of these Iron Age gardens, he found that pulling up the weeds actually caused his harvest to drop. Fertilizer, in the form of animal dung, helped increase yields but was not necessary. Reynolds found that crops grown in less-than-ideal soil conditions using these methods produced two to four tons of food per acre, an incredible accomplishment even for the most high-tech modern farm. The archaeologist is now working on adapting these techniques for use in modern farming. Although his work is still preliminary, he feels that it can be adapted successfully and can release contemporary farmers from their dependence on destructive and dangerous cultivation methods.

Although modern agricultural practices have increased food harvests dramatically in the 20th century, they have also exacted a major toll on the land and must be changed for that land to recover. Another part of the solution to land degradation rests with the consumer. If shoppers insist on vegetables with perfect appearance, farmers will be pressured to use chemicals to produce them. If consumers expect vegetables all through the winter, farmers in warmer climates will be motivated to grow crops year-round instead of letting soils recuperate. If people consume large amounts of meat, livestock production, which is more energy-intensive than crop farming and causes considerable damage to the environment, will continue to expand. If people are willing to change their diet and eating patterns, they will give farmers an incentive for switching to agricultural practices that are less harmful to the earth.

An irrigation canal in California's Central Valley, one of many that enable farmers to grow a multitude of crops in what was once a desert.

chapter 3

IRRIGATION

Most everything in modern agriculture is a mixed blessing, yielding tremendous benefits but at substantial cost. This is perhaps most true of irrigation—the artificial supplying of water to land that would otherwise be too dry for growing crops. Since 1965, the number of acres of irrigated land has almost doubled, from approximately 300 million acres to about 540 million. Although irrigated land gets the least rain and the harshest sunlight and accounts for only 15% of the world's farmed land, it produces more than 30% of the world's food.

Farmers who irrigate their fields can often get two or even three harvests a year, whereas those who rely on natural rainfall usually get only one. Irrigation techniques have also allowed farming to spread to places that would otherwise never have supported it. The most spectacular example of such land transformation is the Central Valley of California. In its natural, unaltered state, this region was a desert, growing little more than sparse junipers and sagebrush. Today, however, it produces a huge amount of vegetables, fruits, and other crops year-round, thanks to the massive rerouting of water from rivers that flow from the mountains in the north. Several western cities depend heavily on artificial water supplies as well, including Los Angeles, California; Phoenix and Tucson, Arizona; and Las Vegas, Nevada.

More than 50 million acres—11% of all U.S. farmland—are irrigated, 90% of them in the western states. Many other regions of the world have come to rely on irrigation as well. Much of the Soviet Union's produce and cotton comes from irrigated land in Soviet Central Asia. In Australia, farming and ranching are almost entirely dependent on irrigation, as is much of agricultural production in China, which has the largest irrigated acreage in the world—about two-thirds of its cultivated land. India also has an extensive irrigation system, especially in the Indus River basin in the north. Since ancient times, Egypt has been completely dependent on irrigation from the Nile River's floodwaters. Altogether, hundreds of millions of people around the world depend on irrigation for their food.

DRAWBACKS TO IRRIGATION

Irrigation has allowed deserts and civilizations to bloom. But it has done so at an immense cost to the land. Worldwide, more than 80 million acres—an area nearly the size of Texas— have been rendered agriculturally sterile by irrigation, and that number is likely to grow much higher soon because of the vast increase in the number of acres recently put under irrigation. Moreover, irrigation has fouled water supplies, rivers, and lakes on an immense scale, killing uncounted numbers of fish, birds, and other animals.

The main culprit in this destruction is salt. Almost all soils contain mineral salts. Some of these are like the table salt everyone is familiar with, but there are many other kinds. All salts

In China's Shandong province, workers dig ditches to transport water to their fields. Two-thirds of this country's cropland is irrigated.

have one thing in common: They kill plants. When conquering armies in ancient times wanted to be sure that a conquered enemy's city never rose to power again, they sowed the land with salt so that nothing could be grown.

Salt dissolves readily in water, and any place where rain falls regularly, salts are periodically washed from the soil into underground water supplies and rivers. But soils in arid lands, which receive little rainfall, contain salts that have accumulated over eons in substantial amounts. This accumulation is not a problem in a natural ecosystem because the salt normally stays deep enough in the ground to be out of the reach of plants. But when land is irrigated and the soil flooded with large amounts of water, that water leaches the salt from the soil, carrying it down into the groundwater supply.

Initially, such leaching is only a minor problem for the farmer, because the groundwater is normally far below the reach of plants' roots. But if the irrigation is continued for a number of years, that constant flow of water overwhelms the system and the water table (the "ceiling" of the groundwater) starts to rise. This rise is accelerated by the high rate of evaporation in desert lands. As surface water evaporates into the air, it leaves what is called a *hydrological vacuum* that in essence sucks up the water from underground. Eventually, this now salt-laden water reaches the surface and the plants' roots, and as it evaporates, it leaves the heavy salt behind at the surface, where it can kill crop plants.

When their crops are threatened by this *salinization*, as salt buildup in soil is called, farmers often try to flush the salt through the soil by flooding it with fresh water. This can work for a short time, but it is only a stopgap measure. Before long, salty groundwater rises again, this time for good, and both the salt and the water, which can drown plant roots—a problem known as *waterlogging*—inflict their damage.

One victim of salt contamination and waterlogging is the Murray Basin in Australia, which produces almost half of that country's food. More than 1 million acres of farmland there have high levels of salt in groundwater that is only 6 feet from the surface and rising fast. Moreover, vast areas of the farmland in Australia are now covered with salt pans (areas where dried salt covers the ground surface).

The Indus River valley in Pakistan and India has an enormous irrigation system—built largely by the British during their control of the region—that covers 30 million acres with almost a million miles of waterways. It is the largest irrigation project in the world. Here also, the groundwater has been rising in some places at the rate of a foot a year, and thus the water table is now less than 10 feet from the surface on more than 55% of the land and nearly 10 million acres have been ruined by salt and waterlogging. To save the remaining land, the government must now build a very expensive drainage system to carry the water away from the area after it has passed through the soil.

Salt and waterlogging are only two of the problems caused by irrigation. Another involves the impact of irrigation on the original water source. In some cases—for instance, in California—irrigation water comes from rivers that are diverted for this purpose. This practice can cause problems because the amount of water available for people—and wildlife—down-stream from the diversion is drastically reduced.

Many of the problems associated with irrigation, in-cluding that of water-source depletion, are frighteningly evident at the Aral Sea in Soviet Central Asia. Once one of the largest inland seas on earth, the Aral has now shrunk to about one-half its original size, destroying wildlife, disrupting the lives of people who used to live on its shores, and causing massive salty dust storms in the surrounding countryside. The problem is that almost all of the water from the rivers that feed the lake has been diverted for cotton growing. The two main rivers that used to feed the sea no longer reach it at all.

This situation, which may be producing the worst environmental disaster in history, is made even worse by the Soviets' cultivation methods. Eager to catch up to Western pro-duction levels, Soviet farmers applied an unheard-of amount of fertilizers, pesticides, and other chemicals to the cotton crops. These chemicals have made their way into the groundwater only to be left behind with the salt when the water rises and evaporates. The desert winds pick up this toxic residue and blow it to surrounding communities. As a result, some two-thirds of the people living around the sea now suffer from one or more devastating illnesses, including throat cancer. The government is now trying to save the sea and its residents, but the cost of this effort is staggering and its success uncertain.

AQUIFER DEPLETION

Rivers are not the only source of water for irrigation. In many places water can be obtained from underground *aquifers*—enormous areas of porous rock that hold water like a sponge. Wells sunk into an aquifer can provide huge, seemingly limitless amounts of water for irrigation. In fact, even the largest aquifers can be and are being depleted. The Ogallala Aquifer in

Water diversion from rivers such as the Colorado can create problems farther downstream—from reduced water flow to salt and pesticide contamination.

Ogallala Aquifer

Wyoming
South Dakota
Nebraska
Colorado
Kansas
Oklahoma
New Mexico
Texas

Aquifer

The Ogallala Aquifer, which flows under eight western states, is the largest in the world, but its water supply is not limitless.

the western United States is a case in point. This vast structure, running under several western states, is the largest in the world. But, like all aquifers, it refills very slowly. If completely emptied, it might take centuries to refill. But in the course of a few decades, farmers over the aquifer have taken a quarter of its water supply, and they continue to pump water out faster than it recharges.

The depletion of this aquifer is bad enough in that it threatens to deprive future farmers of water. It could also have a catastrophic impact on the environment as a whole. Aquifers such as the Ogallala serve as filters and storehouses for the general water supply of the country. If this aquifer dries up, the consequences for lakes and streams thousands of miles away could be disastrous. The ecosystems dependent on those water sources would also be disrupted.

Unfortunately, the only way to deal with aquifer depletion is to limit how much water farmers withdraw from aquifers—that is, to regulate the supply, preventing water from being withdrawn from an aquifer faster than it refills. This strategy can pose difficult legal problems, however, where aquifers are so large that they underlie more than one state. In such cases, regulation must be carried out on a national level.

SOLUTIONS

A variety of strategies can be used to reduce irrigation damage and water waste. One is to build drainage systems that allow water to drain away from fields rather than add to the groundwater. Such systems can make a tremendous difference in preventing environmental damage from irrigation, but they are expensive to install. In the long run, of course, drainage systems actually save money, because they reduce the cost of lost yields and field damage, but most large-scale irrigation systems in developing countries are built with money from development banks that wish to see a quick return on their investment. Drainage systems add to the cost of such an investment but do not show any apparent return for many years, so many irrigation projects do not include them.

Drainage systems also do not solve the problem of water contamination. They drain water from fields only after it has passed through the soil and become salty. This water has to go somewhere. In most cases, it ends up being dumped into the same river that provided the irrigation water in the first place, and farmers and cities downstream get salty river water.

In Los Angeles, for instance, the water comes indirectly from the Colorado River, which passes through a huge number of irrigation projects and gets saltier from each one. In some years, the water is so salty that it exceeds safety limits for drinking. Mexican farmers living along the Colorado's southern extreme get water that is so salty it will kill their crops if they put it on their fields. The Mexican government has had to resort to international negotiations to get the United States to build desalinization (salt-removing) plants at the border.

The best solution to the problems caused by irrigation is to use less water. Most standard irrigation systems, which use unlined ditches to transport water to fields, are terribly inefficient. On average, they deliver to the plants only half the water originally collected; the rest is lost through seepage and evaporation. Sprinkler systems that distribute water through pipes fare better, but the best irrigation method is called *drip irrigation,* in which water is delivered by way of plastic hoses that have holes over the plants, so that a relatively small amount of water is delivered directly to the plant and only when it needs it. Drip systems dramatically reduce water consumption and also improve plant growth because they prevent overwatering.

Although improved irrigation systems cost farmers money, they can increase a harvest enough to pay for themselves quite rapidly. For example, in 1984, the government of Chile tried an experiment in that country's Claro River valley in which the usual flooding and ditch methods of irrigation were replaced with a system of more even water distribution. Farmers monitored the moisture in the soil closely and irrigated only when necessary.

The result, for an investment of $25 to $30 an acre, was an increase in yields of 60%. This was achieved using only the most basic and inexpensive improvements.

Israel is generally considered a model of successful irrigation application. This country's farmers use both drip irrigation and drainage systems, and the government strictly controls the amount of water that can be applied. Moreover, the

A hose circling an almond tree distributes small amounts of water to the soil at four locations. This drip irrigation system uses much less water than do conventional methods.

Israelis have been experimenting with plants that can tolerate higher levels of salt in the soil. Through this approach, they have almost completely avoided the problems of salinization and waterlogging while feeding an ever-increasing population in the midst of a desert.

No irrigation system, including those used in Israel, can completely eliminate environmental problems, but through sensible, responsible management, the adverse effects of irrigation can be minimized.

Clouds of dust and soil rise into the air as an Alabama farmer works a dried-up field during a severe drought in 1986. Where unprotected by vegetation, cropland becomes highly vulnerable to wind erosion.

E R O S I O N

Of all the problems of land degradation, none is as serious as erosion. Erosion occurs when soil is carried away by either water or wind, leaving the land without its fertile topmost layer. If the erosion is extensive enough and occurs over a long enough period of time, the soil can lose its ability to support life. Once that topsoil is gone, it may take centuries to replace.

Erosion is a natural process. Every part of the earth experiences it to one degree or another whenever it rains or the wind blows. In some places, such as the deserts of the American West, even natural erosion can be severe. The Grand Canyon is a spectacular illustration of this phenomenon.

Not all erosion, furthermore, is bad. Egyptian civilization, for instance, flourished for thousands of years thanks to the Nile River valley's fertility, which in turn is the product of silt deposited by the river, which flows north to the Mediterranean Sea from rivers and lakes deep within Africa. Particles of silt are washed into the river by rains or by the river's passage through loose soil. The silt is suspended in the water as long as the river keeps moving. Once it slows down, the particles fall out of suspension and drop to the ground.

This is precisely what happened when the Nile flooded each year as a result of a heavy waterload produced during the rainy season far inland, where the river begins. When the Nile overflowed its banks, the water spread out and was no longer turbulent and the silt settled to the bottom. Then, when the floodwaters receded, the silt was left behind, adding valuable nutrients to the soil. Floodplains such as the Nile's are among the most fertile farmlands on earth. (Unfortunately, the Nile no longer functions as well as it once did. In the 1960s, the Egyptians, in an attempt to control the fluctuating water level that resulted from periodic droughts inland, built the Aswân High Dam to create a reservoir and to provide a reliable water supply for irrigation. Although the dam has helped in that regard, it also disrupted the silt supply system and removed the flushing action of floodwaters that carried away excess salt. Some people now question whether the dam should have been built in the first place.)

In natural erosion, the loss of topsoil usually keeps pace with the natural creation of new topsoil, so that the soil never entirely loses its fertility. But today, because of intensive farming techniques, overgrazing, and deforestation, erosion has leapt far ahead of topsoil replacement, weakening the land in many regions of the world with each successive season.

On average, it takes about 10,000 years for a foot of topsoil to develop naturally, yet every year, many American farms lose a quarter inch of topsoil from every acre. In other words, it takes 10,000 years to make a foot of topsoil and 48 years to lose it through erosion as a result of farming practices. Obviously, at this rate it will not be long before the topsoil, which has an average depth of 15 inches, is gone altogether. Even before it disappears, however, damage can be done. If just 6 inches of topsoil are lost, crop yields can drop by as much as 40%.

Farming techniques vastly accelerate the rate of erosion, but they can also accelerate the pace of topsoil replacement. Through proper plowing and fertilizer application and by leaving fields fallow (without crops for a period of time), farmers can offset some of the damage—but not enough. Every year, there is a worldwide net loss of 24 billion tons of topsoil. The amount lost over the past 10 years alone equals half of all the topsoil on U.S. farmland. Altogether, one-third of all farmland in the world is now suffering severe erosion, with the most serious problems existing in Africa, China, India, Australia, and the Soviet Union. In the United States, 93% of the entire land surface (not just farmland) is suffering from slight to moderate erosion.

Natural erosion has created such spectacular geologic formations as the Grand Canyon in northwestern Arizona.

Farming-induced erosion begins when land is plowed. Plowing itself is not a problem, because it allows water and air to reach the lower levels of the soil, but this effect is a benefit only if the original plant cover grows back immediately. In farming, however, the original plant cover—usually grasses or forest—is replaced by crops. Even when crops are planted densely, they cannot provide as complete a ground cover as does a field of wild grasses.

Fewer plants and thus fewer roots mean less cohesion in the top layer of soil, and less variety of plants means poorer overall soil vitality. The soil loses its resilience and its ability to

Rills created by flowing soil and water traverse eroded slopes in eastern Washington.

hold nutrients and moisture. Also, soil that is exposed to air without the cover of plants can be quickly dried out by the sun, becoming hard and relatively impenetrable, so that when rains come, the water simply runs off the surface instead of being absorbed by the soil. If the water is not absorbed well, the soil loses one of its vital components, and when the water runs off the surface, it can carry with it a good deal of the topsoil. This running water can further damage farmland by creating small channels called rills or steep-sided depressions called gullies. Moreover, when soil does not absorb rainwater and dries up, it loses its cohesion. The little clumps break down into individual particles, and when the wind blows, it picks up those particles and carries them away.

That is exactly what happened on a grand scale during the droughts of the 1930s on the American plains, a region that came to be called the Dust Bowl. The introduction of mechanized tractors earlier in the century coincided with an abnormally wet period in the climate, so that farmers were able to plant more and more crops and produce larger and larger yields. More people moved to the area, hoping to make a lot of money in farming. In the Texas panhandle, for instance, the amount of land planted in wheat rose from 70,000 acres to 1,600,000 acres in just 20 years. Similar scenarios were played out all over the southern plains states, and for about 30 years—with the exception of a drought in 1910—it seemed as if a new Garden of Eden had sprung up.

The climate of this region, however, fluctuates from wet to dry in periods that can last decades. The 30-year wet period in the early 20th century was an example of one of those climate swings. On a human scale, a 30-year cycle is difficult to perceive—if the weather is rainy for 30 years in a row, a whole generation grows up with that standard and will reasonably assume that it will always be rainy. But in terms of global climate, 30 years is only the blink of an eye, and in the late 1920s and early 1930s the weather in the southern plains swung the other way. One dry year followed another until, within a few years, farming became impossible. Under natural circumstances, the soil and the plant life would have survived the drought. But the original ground cover of short prairie grass had been replaced by monocultures of wheat, cotton, and other crops, which left most of the soil surface exposed and vulnerable.

The land had been repeatedly plowed and pulverized and was now being severely dried out, so that when the winds came, all the loose, dry surface soil was picked up and blown across the country, destroying farms and leaving thousands of families without a means of supporting themselves. Whole counties were deserted as people left for the cities, and huge dust storms swept the skies.

This catastrophe spurred the creation in 1935 of the U.S. Department of Agriculture Soil Conservation Service. Initially charged with promoting soil conservation practices in the Great Plains, the agency now operates throughout the country. Since its creation, American farmers have adopted some erosion-prevention methods, but further efforts are needed—soil conservation is currently practiced on only about half of all U.S. farmland.

AFRICAN DUST BOWL

The same drought-induced erosion process that plagued the United States earlier in the century is happening today in

Crouched among his stunted corn crop during the 1930s Dust Bowl, an Indiana farmer scatters a handful of dry topsoil.

Africa, although with fewer tractors. Much of the tilling there is done by hand or with draft animals, but the land has been degraded nonetheless because increasing populations and increasing demand for cash have forced farmers to plant more crops more often. Where they once left any given piece of land fallow for 20 years before returning to cultivate it, economic and social pressures now force them to wait only 5 to 10 years.

That practice means that the soil has less chance to recover from the strain of cultivation. In many places, the destruction is accelerated by overgrazing of animals (see Chapter 6). As a result, experts predict that increasingly infertile land will cause Africa's food production to drop by one-quarter by the year 2000.

In the Sahel of northern Africa—a belt of relatively dry land just below the Sahara desert and running east to west across the African continent—a repetition of the American dust bowl is now playing itself out. In this case, there was no wet period to attract increased agriculture; it was simply a matter of more people on the land coinciding with the introduction of Western agricultural methods—a development known as the Green Revolution.

International aid agencies and banks have in recent decades set up enormous schemes to grow cotton, peanuts, and various other crops on a massive scale. Most of these agencies, being based in Europe and America, employ agricultural experts who were trained in the West, and these experts most often simply transfer their seemingly tried-and-true techniques to Africa. But Africa is not Kansas. The soil in Africa developed in conjunction with different plants, different water cycles, and different insects and microorganisms. Simply planting corn or wheat will not work for long there. Massive amounts of fertilizers and chemicals must be added to the soil to support the crops, and even then, new strains of disease-resistant, higher-yielding plants have to be introduced on a regular basis. All these actions cost a great deal of money, and farmers must work the land harder and harder to earn more. The combination of foreign crops and intensified cultivation puts a strain on the land that it cannot bear.

To make matters worse, the Sahel is subject to regular periodic droughts that can last several years. As in the American Dust Bowl, the native ecosystem can withstand these dry periods, but worn-out soil planted with unsuitable crops and lacking in ground cover cannot. More and more often, winds blowing out of the desert pick up the dried-out soil and gather it in tremendous dust storms.

In China, erosion is both the basis for much of the country's food supply and the single greatest environmental threat. The most densely cultivated region in China is an area called the North China Plain. To the northwest of this plain lies a vast plateau covered in an enormously thick layer of *loess*, a kind of soft, yellowish brown, loamy sediment that is excellent for farming. The loess originates in the central Asian deserts, where it is picked up by winds and carried hundreds of miles until the winds give out over the plateau and drop their sediment. Over eons, this process has built up a layer of loess more than a thousand feet deep, making it the deepest soil on earth.

The Huang He, or Yellow River, runs through this plateau, picking up huge amounts of loess that turn it a muddy yellow (giving the river its name) and carrying this fertile material down to the North China Plain. Loess, being loose, wind-deposited sediment, is very easily eroded by water, either in the form of rivers or rain. As a result, farmers who want to take advantage of its fertility run the risk of losing their fields quite easily. This is just what has happened on a grand scale in China.

Erosion along the Yellow River leads to another problem. The river carries so much sediment—up to 34% of the river's mass—that some of it falls out of suspension as the river flows. As the silt settles out of the water, it drops to the riverbed, and over the years the bed rises in height, as do the banks, which are also built of deposited sediment. The growth of the banks generally keeps the river in check, but every now and then an especially heavy rainy season in the mountains causes the river to overflow its banks and flood the surrounding farmlands.

For centuries the Chinese have faced this threat by constructing dikes, or artificial riverbanks, to hold back the floodwaters. This has worked for the most part, but the cure may be proving worse than the disease. The dikes do keep the river from flooding, but floods are not all bad. As is the case along the Nile in Africa, flooding spreads the Yellow River's heavy silt load over a wide area, enriching the floodplain even as it threatens the towns and farms that rely on that richness. When dikes keep the river within its banks, the sediment that would have been spread across the country in floods stays in the riverbed, causing it to grow higher and higher. The people keep building the dikes higher as well—at the rate of a foot every three years—but in doing so they make potential floods more devastating.

Eventually, the river will reach a critical flood stage, which it has done periodically in history. When it does, it will cause massive devastation. This area of China produces almost a fifth of the country's food and is home to millions of people. A major flood here could cripple China on a scale that it has never seen before. (In fact, sediment buildup poses a similar threat for the Yangtze River in southern China. In 1991, massive flooding during the rainy season caused extensive damage in this region, collapsing dams, wrecking millions of homes, and destroying millions of acres of crops.)

SOLUTIONS

A number of strategies for preventing erosion exist, some of which are based on the general soil conservation methods discussed in Chapter 2. Any farming method that reduces monocropping, for instance, helps increase ground cover and soil vitality and so helps prevent wind and water erosion. In a method called *strip cropping*, for example, strips of crops—such as corn—that expose a lot of soil are alternated with strips of crops—such as alfalfa—that cover the ground more thoroughly. Crop rotation can also help prevent erosion. In addition to restoring nutrients, the planting of ground-covering crops such as legumes and cereal plants in alternate seasons gives the soil better protection than do row crops.

Another soil conservation method that prevents soil loss is *conservation-tillage farming*, in which the topsoil is disturbed as little as possible to hold it together and reduce erosion. Special tillers loosen subsurface soil only, and seeds are injected by machine into the topsoil.

Erosion of sloping cropland can be reduced by a number of methods. One is *contour farming*, in which crops are planted across rather than up and down a slope of land.

Terracing, or cutting slopes into a series of level shelves—somewhat like a giant staircase—can help stop water erosion on very steep hillsides. This farming method is used on many slopes in China, for example, to both hold rainwater and prevent the loss of loess. Each terrace has a small wall around its edge to keep rainwater from running down the hill and carrying away the soil. A recent land restoration program initiated by the Chinese government in the province of Shanxi involved terracing and the planting of fruit and fuelwood trees on the slopes, along with nitrogen-producing shrubs that provide animal fodder in addition to reducing erosion. This program was so successful that between 1979 and 1986, farmers used only half the land that they had used previously and yet produced 17% more food—an increased efficiency of 134%.

Planting trees and hedges along the margins of fields can also help reduce the effects of wind erosion. Hedgerows—strips of wild vegetation that are often left between fields by accidents of plowing and fencing—have the added advantage of helping control pests.

Farmers can even use living organisms to control erosion. One interesting example of this approach exists in Africa, where scientists have recently found that a certain species of termite builds its underground nests in long, parallel rows that rise up

Terraced rice fields in Bali, Indonesia, take on a sort of sculpted splendor. The shelflike slopes of land serve to retain water and prevent erosion.

from the ground like a series of small ridges about four feet high. These ridges serve as natural controls against wind and water erosion. Farmers are finding that planting crops at various heights on the slopes of these ridges gives them very fine control over the amount of sun and water the plants get, thus helping ensure a fuller harvest.

The use of such natural control mechanisms can greatly reduce soil erosion. The ideal approach to erosion control, of course, is to disrupt the land as little as possible and to cultivate only suitable terrain. Unfortunately, because of the growing world population, economic forces, and degradation of once-fertile lands, there is increasing pressure to grow crops and raise animals in unsuitable locations. This pressure contributes to two forms of land degradation discussed in the following chapters: deforestation and desertification.

Forestry officials inspect a "brush check dam," built to halt the erosion of a gully in a Philippine forest that has been damaged by logging, burning, and other harmful activities.

D E F O R E S T A T I O N

In the time it takes to read this sentence, an area of tropical rainforest the size of a football field will have been cut down, and with it will go an unknown number of species of plants and animals and a priceless piece of the earth's biosphere—that part of the earth and its atmosphere inhabited by living things. Every minute of every day, around the clock, around the world, 90 acres of tropical forest are cut down, for a total of more than 40 million acres a year, according to recent estimates. The greatest destruction is occurring in Central and South America, central Africa, and Southeast Asia, but virtually all tropical forests are threatened with deforestation.

Tropical forests are not the only woodlands being destroyed. In the United States, Canada, Chile, and the Soviet Union, vast areas of temperate and boreal forests—those growing in mild and cool climates, respectively—are being cut down at rates almost as alarming as those in the tropics. Each kind of deforestation carries with it serious consequences for the planet.

Most of the deforestation in the tropics—about 60% according to tropical ecologist Norman Myers—is caused by the clearing of forests to make room for farmland or ranching. A smaller but significant percentage of forest—26%—is cut down for timber and wood products. Fuelwood gathering accounts for another 14%. The eventual results of this widespread clearing include soil damage and erosion, the extinction of countless plants and animals, and regional and global climate changes, not to mention the loss of a means of living for indigenous peoples who traditionally reside in forests.

Most rainforest soils are naturally quite thin and infertile, partly because of accidents of geology and partly because the heavy drenching they undergo washes nutrients out of the soil. Plants grow well in them because the plants themselves hold nutrients and water in their trunks, branches, and leaves. The soil really serves only as a base for the trees' roots. Once those roots are removed through deforestation, the soil becomes too weak to stand up to heavy rains.

The result of this deforestation is massive soil erosion, especially on hillsides, so that it becomes even harder for the forest to regrow. Farming is also rendered difficult: Rain washes away most of the soil's already scarce nutrients and minerals, leaving behind high concentrations of iron and aluminum oxides that produce reddish *lateritic* soil, which is difficult to cultivate.

Moreover, with the trees removed, there is little to hold the water when it rains, and tremendous flooding can result, affecting people living far downstream of the actual deforestation site. In 1988 in Thailand, flooding and mud slides caused by deforestation killed more than 400 people and destroyed whole villages. The government there has since passed a ban on logging. India and neighboring Bangladesh have also experienced catastrophic flooding in recent decades, because of deforestation in the Himalayan watershed to the north.

Rainforests such as the Amazon in northern Brazil are being felled at a rapid rate—approximately 90 acres worldwide every minute of every day.

Farmers in the tropics traditionally have cultivated infertile rainforest soil by burning the trees they cut down to allow the nutrients stored in the trees to diffuse into the soil. This practice increases the soil's fertility and makes farming possible, at least for a few years. Then the soil gives out and the farmer moves on to another plot, again clearing the forest and burning the trees. For thousands of years, this has been a successful farming technique in rainforests, one that is generally harmless when it occurs on a small scale. But as larger and larger numbers of people move into the forest and practice this *swidden,* or slash-and-burn, farming, as it is called, the forest has no chance to fully regrow in the abandoned plots before someone else comes along to cut it down. The result is that swidden farming is now the single largest cause of deforestation in the Western Hemisphere and one of the major causes in Asia.

THE LOSS OF SPECIES

Another major consequence of deforestation is species extinction. Tropical rainforests harbor by far the largest percentage of life-forms on earth. Scientists now estimate that these forests may be home to as many as 50 million species, compared with perhaps 8 million in all the rest of the world. A *species* is the smallest category in a system for grouping living things according to their form and genetic structure. Mating between members of the same species can produce fertile young, whereas mating between members of different species cannot. The more species that exist, the greater is the earth's *biodiversity*, or variety of organisms.

Current estimates are that a hundred species become extinct every day worldwide, mostly as a result of tropical deforestation. In the view of Harvard biologist E. O. Wilson, the resultant loss of biodiversity is the single greatest threat to life on this planet. Biodiversity provides the biosphere with genetic flexibility, enabling organisms to survive by adapting to changing conditions.

Species extinction also threatens resources of direct value to humankind. Not only are currently harvested forest products such as hardwood timber endangered, but so are *potential* resources. Rainforest plants already provide the raw materials used in one-fourth of all drugs, and they are believed to contain many more useful medicinal substances, including potential cures for cancer. Unfortunately, the ongoing extinction of tropical species may destroy such lifesaving products before they are discovered. Tropical forests also contain many wild crop strains that can be bred with existing species to increase their yield, heighten their resistance to disease, and produce other improvements. The destruction of these species may endanger the world's food supply by reducing the gene pool from which humans can develop new species.

To understand why there is so much biodiversity in rainforests, it is important to understand how rainforests work. Most forests in temperate and subarctic regions produce a great deal of *biomass*—the total weight of living matter in a given area, including plants and animals—but relatively few species. That is, there are not many different kinds of plants and animals, but there are very large populations of each kind. This situation exists partly because, geologically speaking, glaciers only recently retreated from the northern latitudes—about 10,000 years ago. As a result, species there have had less time to evolve into many different forms. Furthermore, the lack of winter sun, the presence of wide temperature fluctuations, and rocky soils have made life so difficult that only a few species have been hardy enough to survive.

In the tropics, by contrast, the sun shines almost the same amount every day of the year and more intensely than in temperate regions. Temperatures in the tropics are steady and warm, and there tends to be a great deal of moisture in the air. These characteristics together create perfect growing conditions for plants. A large number of plant species, in turn, create the perfect living conditions for a large number of animal species.

In fact, conditions in the tropics are so perfect that plant and animal species struggle to claim a place in the forest, and their competition leads to a great deal of specialization and diversity.

If one species of plant, for example, blooms at night, whereas all others bloom during the daytime, then it will have an edge over its competitors because it has access to a host of otherwise unavailable night-loving pollinators—animals that feed upon flower nectar and carry plant pollen from one plant to another, thereby fertilizing them and enabling them to reproduce. Having exclusive access to certain pollinators means that a plant faces less competition from other species and is more likely to survive and produce offspring with the same unique genetic trait.

Tropical rainforests contain a wealth of species of great potential value to humankind. Continued deforestation threatens to destroy many of these life-forms before all their possible uses are known.

As this process of *evolution,* or genetic adaptation, continues over eons, with each generation becoming more specialized than the last, the rainforest becomes more diverse. Such specialization, however, does have a price. With so many different species growing together, any given species may occur only sporadically and in relatively few numbers. An acre of rainforest might contain several hundred different species of tree, for example, but only one individual of any particular species. In fact, a tree's nearest relative may be half a mile away. That means that pollinators may have a difficult time finding the next representative of that species.

Recent research by Roger Kitching and Meg Lowman, of the University of New England in Australia, and other scientists suggests that because rainforest tree species are sometimes so far apart and the insects on them so specialized, each individual tree may be essentially an island in a sea of foreign trees. An insect on that tree cannot pass over the great distances to the next similar tree, so it stays put. And, just as happens on oceanic islands, a species that is isolated from its kind begins to develop its own evolutionary path, eventually becoming a distinct species. The researchers speculate that each *individual* tree in the rainforest may house a collection of organisms that are found nowhere else on earth. If this is true, then the number of species of life-forms in the world may in fact be even higher than 50 million.

Whatever the total number of species, the rainforest is clearly a highly interdependent and vulnerable habitat, in which the population decline or extinction of one species can spell the doom of others that are dependent on it. Thus, the clearing of even a small area of rainforest may bring about the extinction of a huge number of species and the loss of untold genetic resources.

DEFORESTATION AND
CLIMATE CHANGE

The destruction of tropical forest can also have a major impact on weather, affecting rainfall and temperatures locally and even globally. Recent research has shown, for example, that the rain that gives a rainforest its unique character may be produced by the forest itself. Studies in Brazil showed that only 50% of the rain that falls on the forest comes from clouds formed over the ocean or areas outside the rainforest. The other half of the rain is produced by water that evaporates from leaves of rainforest trees during the heat of the day and forms clouds overhead, which eventually return the water to the forest.

Although such studies have so far been limited to Brazil, it is likely that these findings also apply to rainforests in other areas. This means that cutting large areas of rainforest may reduce the overall amount of water that is taken up during the day in a particular region, and what forest is still standing may not get enough rain. If that happens, then that section of forest will die, even though it has not itself been cut, thus reducing even further the amount of water taken up and released as rain and making the problem even worse. This kind of system, where one negative action worsens conditions enough to produce greater and greater destructive effects, is called *negative feedback*.

Another reason that people are concerned about losing rainforests is that these forests absorb a great deal of carbon dioxide. Carbon dioxide is the most abundant of the so-called greenhouse gases, which scientists fear are trapping the earth's heat and increasing the temperature of the planet's atmosphere. In a process known as photosynthesis, plants of all kinds take in

Once abundant throughout Haiti, tropical forests have all but vanished in this Latin American country because of rampant deforestation, as this aerial photograph attests.

carbon dioxide and release oxygen, just as humans breathe in oxygen and breathe out carbon dioxide. Using energy from sunlight, a plant combines carbon from carbon dioxide with hydrogen from water to make carbohydrates, which provide food for the plant's growth; the carbon itself becomes incorporated into the plant's tissues. Oxygen, the by-product of this reaction, is released into the atmosphere through pores in the plant's leaves.

Because industrial society produces a great deal of carbon dioxide, there is more need than ever for green plants that can absorb this gas and store the carbon. When rainforests are cut and burned, a huge portion of this carbon bank is released, contributing to global warming. The scale of swidden farming is now so vast, in fact, that the carbon dioxide released by this agricultural practice is significantly adding to the greenhouse effect, even as the trees that would normally store excess carbon are removed. Together, these problems are estimated to add 2.8 billion metric tons of carbon to the atmosphere each year, representing one-third of all the carbon released by humans (second only to industrial and car exhausts). It might seem that the grass and other vegetation that replace the forest would take over the forest's carbon-absorbing function, but forests store 20 to 100 times as much carbon as do grasses and crops.

Tropical deforestation also adds to the greenhouse effect in another, less obvious way—by increasing the population of insects called termites. Termites are extremely abundant in rainforests, building their nests on tree trunks or in mounds on the ground and eating wood of all kinds—especially dead wood. Their function is a helpful one in rainforests, because they recycle the nutrients in fallen trees quickly. But like most creatures that eat plant material, they cannot easily break down the cellulose that gives plants their rigidity. So the termites rely on bacteria in their guts to chemically dissolve the cellulose. The major by-product of this chemical reaction is methane, which a termite releases as gas in what amounts to a termite burp. This tiny event is normally so small as to be insignificant. But when it is multiplied by billions upon billions of termites eating nonstop, the methane that is produced becomes very significant indeed.

Methane, although less abundant in the earth's atmosphere than carbon dioxide, reflects far more heat, so that in terms of the greenhouse effect, increased methane is even more of a concern than increased carbon dioxide. And with 40 million acres of forest cut down each year, there are far more dead trees, providing food for far more termites, who collectively release far more methane. Scientists now estimate that termites alone add 40 million tons of this gas to the atmosphere each year. Cattle add even more methane to the atmosphere than do termites, and much of the land that is cleared in rainforests is done so for cattle ranching, thus compounding the problem.

NONTROPICAL FORESTS

Deforestation is not limited to the tropics or to rainforests. It is also occurring in the huge boreal forests that stretch across Canada, Scandinavia, and the Soviet Union, totaling 6 million square miles of predominantly coniferous (cone-bearing) evergreen trees, mostly pine, cedar, fir, and spruce. These forests are remarkably uniform around the world, with almost identical species in Siberia and Ontario. Although the number of species in these northern forests is far smaller than that estimated to

Cattle roam through barren pasture that has replaced a once lush Amazonian rainforest.

exist in tropical forests (27,000 as compared to 20 million), the biomass—and so the amount of carbon stored in this type of forest—is much higher, twice that of a rainforest.

The amount of this forest that is cleared each year is nearly as great as that cleared in the tropics. In Canada, for example, there are approximately 1,500,000 square miles of forest, of which 90,000 square miles have been cleared without being replanted. The Amazon rainforest, at 1,200,000 square miles, has lost 151,000 square miles. Because the species of northern forests are so widespread and have such large populations, this forest clearing is not likely to result in major extinctions, and because the soil is much more stable to begin with, erosion is not as serious a problem in northern regions as it is in the tropics. However, because they store such a large

Vacationers stop to admire the scenery in the Yukon, in Canada. Although less endangered than tropical forests, boreal forests in Canada and other northern climates are dwindling, in large part because of logging.

amount of carbon, clearing of boreal forests may contribute significantly to global warming.

Also threatened with destruction are the temperate forests in South America along the coast of Chile, which are being cut at tremendous rates. These woods are actually rainforests, but temperate rainforests of cedar and other conifers that thrive in cold, wet climates. They hold an even greater biomass than boreal forests and so contain even larger amounts of carbon— the highest in the world.

Temperate deciduous forests are located in regions such as the eastern United States that have moderate climates with four distinct seasons. These forests contain such trees as oak, hickory, maple, and beech all of which shed their leaves at the end of each growing season. Temperate forests are commonly cleared for timber, agricultural use, and urban development, but they grow back more easily than tropical forests. These forests are increasingly threatened, however, by air pollution, especially acid rain produced by fossil fuel burning, which weakens trees and makes them susceptible to disease and other environmental stresses.

SOLUTIONS TO DEFORESTATION

Forests around the world are cleared for different reasons and with different effects, and saving them requires different strategies, ranging from replanting to sustainable-use forestry projects to outright protection from development. These measures can only succeed, however, if the economic pressures driving deforestation are addressed. In the tropics, especially, the

Replanting trees is vital to the preservation of boreal and temperate forests.

combined pressures of population growth and poverty tend to encourage deforestation for short-term profit.

The cutting of boreal forests for wood products can be slowed if consumers of these products reduce their demand. Much of that demand is for paper. Newspapers, magazines, books, copying machines, and mail advertising all use enormous amounts of paper, and production of all of these goods must be reduced drastically if these forests are to survive. Reforestation— that is, planting trees to replace the ones cut—also needs to be carried out on a larger scale and with greater emphasis on diversity. (Most forest plantations favor one type of tree to facilitate harvesting.) Currently, many forestry companies may log public forest lands for their timber and so have little impetus to reseed these plots. Another strategy for reducing the demand for wood is to recycle paper products, a practice that has become more widespread in recent years and is increasingly required by law.

In areas where forests are cut for cropland, one of the most promising developments is *agroforestry*, a practice in which farmers plant trees among their crops. When this system is properly managed, the trees help restore nutrients to the soil, control water flow and erosion, and provide shade for crops that need it, while also giving farmers a source of firewood. This system gives farmers an alternative to forest clearing for fuelwood. In one such project, in southern Guatemala, the organization CARE (Cooperative for American Relief Everywhere) International is planting more than 50 million trees over a period of 10 years. In addition to their agricultural benefits, these trees will soak up 15 million tons of carbon.

One of the more unusual programs to relieve tropical deforestation at first appears to have nothing at all to do with trees. In Costa Rica, a woman named Dagmar Werner, working with the Smithsonian Tropical Research Institute, is raising large native lizards called iguanas for food. The tail meat of the iguana is considered a delicacy in Central America. Werner's hope is that these iguanas can replace the cattle that currently produce most of the meat in the tropics. Cattle, although a good source of protein, are inefficient users of rainforest land. Trees have to be cleared to raise them, but the cleared land can support grass for only about seven years, and then new land has to be cleared.

Iguanas, on the other hand, need intact rainforest to survive. By hand-raising hatchlings until they can survive on their own in the forest, farmers can raise the animals in densities that produce as much meat per acre as cattle. Werner believes that this system, if carried out on a large scale, could replace cattle

Iguana ranching is one of a number of promising sustainable forestry projects now under way in the tropics. The meat of this lizard is considered a delicacy.

ranching, give farmers an equally profitable venture, and, most importantly, give local people an economic incentive to preserve the lizard's forest habitat. The one hurdle remaining is the creation of a market for iguana meat. Although it is a delicacy, iguana meat is not considered an everyday food item by most people, and whereas there is an international demand for beef and an international distribution network to buy it, iguana meat must still be sold to one store owner at a time.

Other sustainable-use projects in the tropics include one exploring the possibility of raising pacas, a large native rodent with flesh said to taste like pork. In another venture, people are experimenting with new forestry methods, including planting fast-growing trees such as legumes, particularly one called *Acacia mangium.* The aim of this plan is to replant forests and provide a profit-making alternative to cutting down virgin forests. Projects such as these are especially promising because they address not only biological problems but also the economic problems that are the driving force behind deforestation. If they can be duplicated and carried out on a worldwide basis, there may be real hope for preserving the world's forests.

The combination of drought and wind have transformed this wheat field into a desertlike wasteland.

chapter 6

DESERTIFICATION

For most people the word *desert* conjures up images of
sand dunes, rock, and waterless desolation, a place where hardly
anything can live. But there is more than one kind of desert. There
are natural deserts, ranging from the hot, giant sand dunes of the
Sahara to the cold rock deserts of Mongolia to, strangely enough,
the ice deserts of Antarctica, which can be considered desert because they get so little precipitation—it almost never snows there.
All of these habitats are technically deserts even though they are
radically different kinds of places. All of them are natural, self-
sustaining ecosystems, and all support a surprising amount of life.

But there is another, new kind of desert, where life does
not exist in abundance, a desert made by humans that is eating up
a large part of the world. Every year, this type of desert grows by
another 80,000 square miles—an area as big as New Mexico.
Once it is destroyed, much of this land cannot be reclaimed but
will remain desert forever. *Desertification*, the process by which
land becomes desert, affects a huge amount of land: The United
Nations estimated at its 1977 conference on desertification that
11 million square miles of the earth's surface—an area almost 3
times as large as the entire United States—are threatened with this

problem. It is occurring mostly in arid and semiarid regions, particularly in Africa, south-central Asia, the western United States, Australia, and the southern portion of South America.

The causes of desertification include deforestation, overgrazing, overcultivation, and inappropriate irrigation practices, which as described earlier can lead to salinization and waterlogging, potentially creating a salty desert. Desertification is increasing in large part because more and more people are living on semiarid lands. These habitats are somewhere between a grassland and desert in terms of rainfall, climate, and vegetation. They usually support short grasses, shrubs, and even some trees, and they often support many animals. The high plains of the United States in the western parts of Nebraska, Kansas, Texas, and the Dakotas, as well as the eastern parts of Colorado, New Mexico, Wyoming, and Montana are good examples of this kind of habitat. There are also extensive semiarid regions in Asia, the Soviet Union, and Africa. These areas get some rain—not enough to grow crops but enough to support animals and some people.

Traditionally, people living in semiarid lands have been herders, or people who keep cattle, sheep, and goats. Until recently there were few of these herders, because semiarid regions are fairly harsh. The people dwelling there traditionally led simple lives, living on their animals' meat and milk and trading meat and milk with neighbors for the few things they could not provide on their own.

Under light occupancy, this kind of land use can work indefinitely. But 30 or 40 years ago, when the world's political and economic order began to alter, more and more people began moving onto semiarid lands. After World War II, colonial empires dissolved, national boundaries were altered, roads were built, jet travel was introduced, cities sprang up in places that never had them before, electricity and technology reached into the countryside, and the general standard of living around the world went up. In addition, beginning in the 1970s, American and European banks began loaning huge sums of money to developing countries in Latin America, Africa, and Asia.

The growth of human-made deserts has been produced by two aspects of all this change: population growth and money. The human population, which has grown at a disturbing rate of 1.7% to 2.1% annually since mid-century, has grown even faster in developing nations. The population of the African continent, for example, has been increasing at a rate of almost 3% annually and is expected to double in only 24 years, according to ecologist and population expert Paul Ehrlich.

Much of this growing African population initially migrated to cities, but before long, people began spilling out of the overcrowded cities and into the surrounding countryside. But when they reached the countryside, there were already people there, so some of the newcomers went farther and some of the

Sheepherders have inhabited the steppes of Soviet Central Asia for centuries. Such semi-arid regions are increasingly threatened by overgrazing.

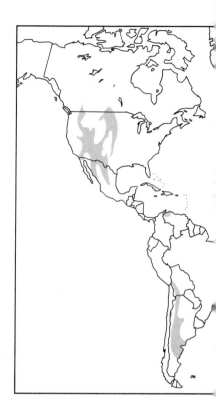

Approximately 11 million square miles of the earth's surface are threatened with desertification, according to United Nations estimates.

original residents were displaced and had to move. Like people freely filling a theater—where the good seats get taken first, then the ones on the aisles, and finally the ones in the balcony—the semiarid lands (the equivalent of balcony seats) were taken last. Nobody wanted to be there, but all the better land was taken—often by wealthy plantation farmers—and the cities were too crowded.

Because the only practical way to make a living on semiarid land is to herd cattle, sheep, and goats, that is what all the newcomers did, and it was not long before there were many more animals on the land than ever before—more than the land

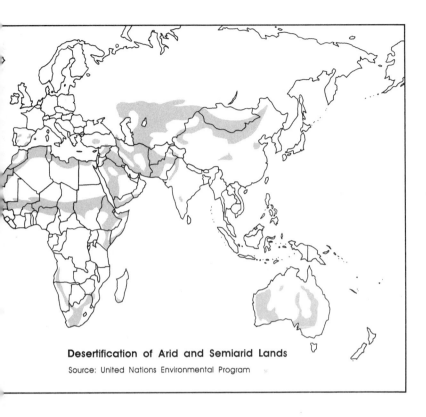

Desertification of Arid and Semiarid Lands
Source: United Nations Environmental Program

could support. This problem would be bad enough in itself, but it was made even worse by the introduction of money.

Until the past few decades, people in semiarid lands, as in many remote areas, lived without money. They traded goods for the things they needed, or they provided for themselves. But as jets and roads and bank investments made their way into the more remote regions, people began using cash for their transactions. In themselves, cash economies are not necessarily bad, but they are tied to regional and international economics rather than to local circumstances and so are generally beyond the control of the herder or crop grower. Furthermore, the cash economies in developing nations are linked to—and in many ways governed by—the immense debt of these countries. The farmers in indebted nations are encouraged to grow cash crops for export rather than *staple crops,* or those intended for local consumption. When many nations adopt this strategy, worldwide overproduction results, causing prices to fall.

When such overproduction occurs—as it frequently does—a cattle herder receives less money for his or her cows. The herder still has children to feed and clothe, however, and so puts more cattle on the land in order to sell more cattle to make more money. But all the herders in the region are in the same plight, and they all put more animals on the land. Before long the animals eat everything in sight; the vegetation disappears, and the topsoil, which the vegetation was holding in place, blows away. Once again, when the topsoil is gone, nothing can grow on that land, and it takes centuries for the topsoil to be replaced. The only thing the animals do not eat are the trees. Cattle, sheep, and goats are grazing animals, which means they eat grasses, not trees or shrubs. There are not many trees in this kind of landscape, but the ones that are there serve to hold the soil in place and function as homes for birds and other animals. Unfortunately, although the cattle and sheep do not destroy the trees, the people do. People in such regions cannot ordinarily afford to buy gas or other fuel. They have to do all their cooking on wood fires, and the only way to get wood is to cut down those few trees. Again, with more people on the land, more trees get cut than usual, and the trees that were holding the soil soon disappear altogether.

People then turn to cattle dung (manure) for fuel. Dung does not burn as well as wood, but when dried it will make a fire. This would not be a problem except that cattle dung is one of the best fertilizers for the soil, and soil that is already suffering overgrazing and woodcutting needs fertilizer more than ever, so losing the dung to fires robs the soil just when it needs help most.

SOLUTIONS TO DESERTIFICATION

One solution to desertification is to replant trees and seed grasses on damaged lands, and this approach is currently being tried on a large scale in China. Although this strategy works in the short run, it does not address the fundamental cause of the problem in most developing countries. Thus, replanted trees are likely to be cut down 10 years later.

In general, the economic problems that drive desertification must be addressed on an international level. Because the money a herder receives for exported cattle is part of a huge global market, international laws and agreements are needed to help smooth over the economic fluctuations—caused by such factors as changing interest rates—that have such a devastating

A farmer in northern Ethiopia tries to work the soil during a period of severe drought that has made cultivation almost impossible.

impact on the local level. The governments of developing nations should also be discouraged from establishing subsidies and tax incentives that encourage overgrazing and other causes of desertification.

Some of the strategies for combating desertification may not seem to have anything at all to do with the land but may be essential for saving it. For example, one way to stop desertification—and land degradation in general—is to teach women to read. Because a big part of the problem is population growth, it is essential to reduce the number of children born, and one of the best ways to do that is to provide education—especially for women. A recent study in Asia by the World Bank indicated that when the number of women receiving a secondary school education doubled, the birthrate dropped by 30%. The study's findings suggest that a woman who learns to read will likely get a better understanding of the problems and possibilities she

In rural Bangladesh, a family planning council run by the Save the Children Federation provides villagers with birth control and other health care information that will help them build a better life.

faces—such as birth control options—and will often choose not to have as many children. Also, the children she does have will get better care.

In addition, researchers have recently found that because of some little-known biological controls naturally built into the human reproductive system, new mothers are less likely to become pregnant again as long as they are producing milk for a breastfeeding baby. So if mothers increase the amount of time they breastfeed their babies, they may increase the time between bearing children and thus reduce the number of children they will have. Although not foolproof, this method is an inexpensive, natural form of birth control that anyone can practice. Encouraging it will require education, however, because many women in developing countries think that breastfeeding is old-fashioned and would rather use bottled formula.

Another promising, although controversial, idea for combating desertification is that of biologist Alan Savory, who runs a nonprofit organization in Albuquerque, New Mexico, called the Center for Holistic Resource Management. Savory has developed a method for managing natural resources that he says can stop desertification and even reverse its effects in some cases. His approach is startling because he maintains that the problem in many desertification scenarios is not too many animals on the land, but too few.

Savory developed his ideas while working as a park ranger in Africa. There, he noticed, semiarid grasslands such as the Serengeti Plain support millions upon millions of grazing wild animals, such as wildebeest, and yet the land does not become desertified. Just the opposite: It supports some of the lushest, greenest grass in the world. In North America, too, he realized, millions of bison and antelope once lived on the Great Plains without causing any ill effects on the land. But when humans put even a few thousand cattle on the same kind of land, it quickly turns to desert.

Given the natural system's model, it seemed unlikely that the animals themselves were the problem; cattle do not eat very differently than bison. And the land itself was not any different in the two situations. Therefore, Savory reasoned, the problem must lie in the way the cattle and the land interact. That set him thinking about how ecosystems of land and animals work.

People tend to think of plants and animals as two separate kingdoms, each following its own separate development over time. But plants and animals evolve together. On a given piece of land, with given climatic conditions, only certain kinds of plants can grow, and only certain animals can eat them. For example, in semiarid lands there may be a fair amount of rainfall (some areas that are technically desert actually get 40 inches of rain a year—about the same as Boston), but it does not fall evenly. It tends to come in cloudbursts, or all in one season. That causes problems for plants. In places with a lot of evenly falling rain, plants decompose biologically. When leaves fall from a tree or blades of grass are cut, they are quickly broken down by bacteria and fungi. This decomposition process requires a lot of moisture, however, and in semiarid lands, there is not much. The air has very low humidity and rain is sporadic, so plants that live there have evolved a different strategy to replace their old leaves. In semiarid lands, the plants tend to be grasses, and in this climate their leaf blades decay chemically. They oxidize, or react with oxygen in the air—in effect rusting.

But they oxidize first at the tips of the leaves, and the leaf cannot grow as long as that dead, oxidized part remains there. If the leaf cannot grow, the plant dies—it must be grazed to grow.

Grazing animals that "mow" such grasses thus help the plants to grow; this mutual dependency explains why both grazers and grasses flourished on the American prairies and on the Serengeti Plain. It would seem, then, that cattle would be good for plants in semiarid lands, and yet the plants there die when cattle eat them. Savory reasoned that the only difference between wild animals and domestic cattle is that wild animals move in tightly packed herds. They herd for protection from predators such as lions and leopards, but their herding actually has a side benefit for the land.

Wild animals are constantly on the move and constantly eating. That combination means that when a herd comes pounding through a particular area, they eat the grasses that need trimming, and their hooves break up the dried crust of the earth so that when the rain comes it can get deep into the soil and reach plants' roots; furthermore, the animals drop tons of dung for fertilizer. They then move on, enabling the land to recover.

This is exactly what cattle on a ranch do not do. Because ranchers kill the predators, the cattle do not need to herd together for protection and instead spread out. They do not need to run from predators or move to new grazing areas, and as a result they tend to compact the soil rather than break it up, and the earth develops a hard cap, so that when it does rain, the water simply runs off the surface without getting to plants' roots. And with the cattle spread out, the plants are not all eaten and so begin to die of neglect. Or worse yet, because they do not move far, the cattle

Huge herds of zebra and wildebeest thrive on Africa's Serengeti Plain. New research suggests that this type of land can also support millions of livestock without damage.

keep coming back to the same plants before those grasses have had a chance to recover, so what they do eat tends to become overgrazed.

A rancher whose grazing land degrades will understandably reason that there is not enough feed for the cattle and will remove some of the animals from the fields. But that only makes the situation worse, because then there are even fewer cattle to trim plants, break up land, and fertilize the soil. In this kind of situation, Savory suggests, even vast, sparsely populated grazing areas such as those in the American West can suffer from desertification.

The answer to the problem, according to Savory, is to *increase* the number of cattle or sheep or goats on the land and to find ways to keep them herding together and moving. If a herder watches his land carefully and moves his animals before overgrazing takes place, he should be able to run many more animals on the land than was thought possible. In fact, Savory claims, the more animals the better, an idea that is especially promising for overpopulated lands, where people need more animals. Savory has tried his method with success in a number of countries and has found that it can even reverse the effects of desertification, because when water finally reaches long-buried, dormant seeds, plants spring to life—even after the seeds have been buried 50 or 75 years.

The amount of land threatened with desertification will undoubtedly increase as the human population grows—and with it the demand for food. At the same time, however, farmers and scientists are acquiring a better understanding of the process of desertification and are developing strategies for halting and even reversing it. With more careful land use, exploration of new farming methods, and national and international economic policies that promote more sensible agricultural practices, this form of land degradation may yet be curbed.

Crowds throng a food and merchandise market in Cairo, Egypt. As the world population increases, so will the demand for food and the strain on the earth's resources.

A   T I M E   F O R   C H A N G E

The natural resources of the earth are immense but not inexhaustible, and human activities are taking an increasing toll on these resources. Land degradation, a problem that has received less attention in recent years than has global warming or the depletion of the ozone layer, is nevertheless a serious and growing threat to human survival.

At the same time that the human population and its food requirements are increasing, the amount of cropland is shrinking—by some 15 million acres annually—because of erosion, salinization, desertification, and urban development. Recent statistics compiled by the Worldwatch Institute indicate that global food production may soon be unable to keep pace with the population increase. One indicator of food supplies, world grain production per capita (per person), dropped 14% between 1984 and 1988. This decline was caused partly by droughts but also by a decline in grain acreage, largely as a result of land degradation.

Droughts, furthermore, may increase in coming years if a global warming occurs, as most scientists predict. Higher temperatures are expected to cause or contribute to numerous problems, including desertification in some regions of the world, thus making food production even more difficult.

Bringing about sustainable land use will clearly involve addressing related environmental problems, as well as the issue of population growth. Furthermore, as suggested throughout this book, such a change will require addressing the economic problems that drive so much land degradation, including the huge Third World debt. There is reason to hope, however, that land degradation can be halted before it is too late. There appears to be a growing worldwide awareness of the potential threat posed by modern farming practices, deforestation, and desertification, as well as a growing interest in solving these problems.

The best long-term solutions to land degradation take local economic realities into account. Raising iguanas can only work as a strategy to save rainforests if farmers can find a market for the animals. New crop-planting techniques can be implemented only if farmers can do so without losing money. Banks that finance the building of large-scale irrigation schemes must be convinced of the long-term savings inherent in proper drainage systems as opposed to the purely short-term profits of destructive surface flooding.

Halting land degradation will ultimately require that the global community adopt a more long-term approach to land use. This will require reevaluating international trade agreements, economic and political systems, and even cultural beliefs, as well as developing a new model for the exchange of goods based on the notion of preserving the earth's resources—in other words, developing a *sustainable economy.*

One of the essential components of this idea is that businesses take into account the relationship of resource use and

Prolonged drought turns fertile soil into a shriveled, cracked wasteland.

abuse to long-term profits and losses. Such an approach involves producing "green" products, or those that are good for the environment, not simply to lure consumers but also to protect the earth's resources in the interests of long-term sustainability. Farmers are beginning to understand this concept very well as they discover that pesticides and other seeming advances in modern farming are reducing the long-term productivity of the very soil on which they depend.

The idea of sustainable land use is beginning to catch on. In the mountainous region of India, for example, local people have begun a movement called Chipko, which puts a higher value on intact forests than on timber products. The local farmers have realized that the forest is responsible for holding water, stopping erosion, and protecting soil, and that the money that comes from timber is short-term profit that cannot replace the income lost when fields are degraded because of lost forests. The Chipko movement has brought farmers from all over the Indian Himalayas together to help stop logging operations.

More responsible land use can also be brought about with the proper kind of financial assistance. One grass roots effort designed to give poor farmers an opportunity to implement better agricultural methods and achieve financial independence is the Grameen Bank. This village-based financial assistance program was set up in Bangladesh in 1976 to loan money to poor, landless farmers—mostly women. (In Bangladesh, women grow 50% of the country's food yet receive only 10% of the country's income.)

The Grameen Bank was established to provide money on a short-term basis. Each client can borrow up to $160 at a low interest rate, which they must pay back within a year. Instead of collateral, the bank insists that each borrower join with four others and refuses further loans until all five have repaid their debts. This form of peer pressure not only ensures the loans are repaid quickly but also encourages the villagers to pool their resources to finance a larger project. The groups also meet to conduct bank business and to discuss such matters as birth control. In its first 6 years, the Grameen Bank established 300

Mothers and children wait for vitamins and milk at a rural cooperative near Dhaka, Bangladesh. Financial assistance projects such as the Grameen Bank help alleviate poverty and bring about more sustainable land use.

branches, mostly serviced by bicycle-riding bank officers who come directly to the villages, and loaned $47 million. It also had a lower default rate than any commercial bank. (A default occurs when a borrower fails to repay a loan.) Village income increased 43% on average, and the money helped start countless small agricultural businesses, village shops, and other enterprises that helped alleviate poverty, increase people's self-esteem, and decrease stress on the land. Similar models are now in practice in Malawi, Ivory Coast, Mali, and Tanzania.

Another approach to combating land degradation fueled by economic pressures is the *debt-for-nature* swap. Environmental organizations purchase some of an indebted nation's debt at a discount and sell that reduced debt to the debtor nation if the country promises to implement certain environmental measures, such as wilderness protection. Such debt-for-nature exchanges have been carried out in Bolivia, the Philippines, Ecuador, and Costa Rica by groups including Conservation International and the World Wildlife Fund.

Halting land degradation is no easy challenge. It will require considerable changes in farming methods and other activities as well as in political and economic systems. But it is time for change. Fertile lands are dwindling, and deforestation and desertification are rampant. As the human population of this planet increases, so will strain on the land. Yet there are ways to save it, from improved agricultural practices to sustainable forestry programs to carefully designed financial assistance for developing nations. If such changes are implemented throughout the world, the land may yet be restored and life may flourish for ages to come.

APPENDIX: FOR MORE INFORMATION

Environmental Organizations

Conservation Foundation
1250 24th Street NW
Washington, DC 20037
(202) 293-4800

Global Releaf
c/o The American Forestry
  Association
P.O. Box 2000
Washington, DC 20013
(202) 667-3300

Institute for Alternative
  Agriculture
9200 Edmonston Road, Suite 117
Greenbelt, MD 20770
(301) 441-8777

National Audubon Society
950 Third Avenue
New York, NY 10022
(212) 832-3200

National Coalition Against the
  Misuse of Pesticides
530 Seventh Street SE
Washington, DC 20003
(202) 543-5450

Natural Resources Defense
  Council
40 West 20th Street
New York, NY 10011
(212) 727-2700

Rainforest Action Network
301 Broadway
San Francisco, CA 94133
(415) 398-4404

Rodale Press
33 East Minor Street
Emmaus, PA 18098
(215) 967-5171

Sierra Club
530 Bush Street
San Francisco, CA 94108
(415) 981-8634

Soil and Water Conservation
  Society
7515 Northeast Ankeny Road
Ankeny, IA 50021-9764
(515) 289-2331

World Resources Institute
1709 New York Avenue NW
Washington, DC 20036
(202) 638-6300

Zero Population Growth
1400 16th Street NW
Washington, DC 20036
(202) 332-2200

U.S. Department of Agriculture
14th Street and
 Independence Avenue SW
Washington, DC 20250
(202) 447-2791

C o n v e r s i o n   T a b l e

(From U.S./English system units to metric system units)

Length

1 inch = 2.54 centimeters
1 foot = 0.305 meters
1 yard = 0.91 meters
1 statute mile = 1.6 kilometers (km.)

Area

1 square yard = 0.84 square meters
1 acre = 0.405 hectares
1 square mile = 2.59 square km.

Liquid Measure

1 fluid ounce = 0.03 liters
1 pint (U.S.) = 0.47 liters
1 quart (U.S.) = 0.95 liters
1 gallon (U.S.) = 3.78 liters

Weight and Mass

1 ounce = 28.35 grams
1 pound = 0.45 kilograms
1 ton = 0.91 metric tons

Temperature

1 degree Fahrenheit = 0.56 degrees
 Celsius or centigrade, but to
 convert from actual Fahrenheit
 scale measurements to Celsius,
 subtract 32 from the Fahrenheit
 reading, multiply the result by 5,
 and then divide by 9. For example,
 to convert 212° F to Celsius:

$$212 - 32 = 180 \times 5 = 900 \div 9 = 100° C$$

FURTHER READING

Batie, Sandra S. *Soil Erosion: Crisis in America's Croplands?* Washington, DC: Conservation Foundation, 1983.

Brady, Nyle C. *The Nature and Properties of Soils.* New York: Macmillan, 1974.

Brown, Lester, et al. *State of the World.* New York: Norton, Annual.

Caufield, Catherine. *In the Rainforest.* Chicago: University of Chicago Press, 1984.

Dover, Michael, and Lee Talbot. *To Feed the Earth: Agro-Ecology for Sustainable Development.* Washington, DC: World Resources Institute, 1987.

Doyle, Jack. *Altered Harvest: Agriculture, Genetics, and the Fate of the World's Food Supply.* New York: Viking Press, 1985.

Dregnue, Harold E. *Desertification of Arid Lands.* New York: Academic Press, 1983.

Ehrlich, Paul, and Anne Ehrlich. *Extinction: Causes and Consequences of the Disappearance of Species.* New York: Random House, 1981.

Ellis, William S. "California's Harvest of Change." *National Geographic* (February 1991): 48–73.

Gips, Terry. *Breaking the Pesticide Habit.* Minneapolis: IASA, 1987.

Grainger, Alan. *Desertification: How People Make Deserts, How People Can Stop and Why They Don't.* Washington, DC: Earthscan, 1983.

McDermott, Jeanne. "Some Heartland Farmers Just Say No to Chemicals." *Smithsonian* (April 1990): 114–27.

Myers, Norman. *Gaia: An Atlas of Planet Management.* New York: Doubleday, 1984.

National Research Council. *Alternative Agriculture.* Washington, DC: National Academy Press, 1989.

Olson, Gerald W. *Soils and the Environment: A Guide to Their Applications.* New York: Routledge, Chapman and Hall, 1982.

Paddock, Joe, et al. *Soil and Survival: Land Stewardship and the Future of American Agriculture.* San Francisco: Sierra Club Books, 1987.

Sampson, R. N. *Farmland or Wasteland: A Time to Choose.* Emmaus, PA: Rodale Press, 1981.

Tompkins, Peter, and Christopher Bird. *Secrets of the Soil.* New York: HarperCollins, 1989.

Wilson, Edward O. *Biodiversity.* Washington, DC: National Academy Press, 1988.

GLOSSARY

agroforestry   Planting trees among crops to help restore nutrients to the soil, control **erosion** and water flow, and provide shade for crops.

aquifer   Porous, underground rock or a rock formation that creates a natural underground reservoir that holds **groundwater.**

biodiversity   The genetic variety of living species; the more different species there are, the greater the degree of biodiversity.

biomass   Plant or animal matter used as fuel; also used to refer to the total weight of living matter in a given area.

contour farming   Agricultural method in which crops are planted across—instead of up and down—a slope to prevent erosion.

crop rotation   The planting of nutrient-depleting crops one year and nutrient-restoring plants the next year; increases the fertility of the soil by replenishing nutrients as well as reducing erosion.

desertification   Process by which cultivable land becomes desert, accompanied by a 10% or greater decrease in agricultural productivity; caused by deforestation, drought, overgrazing, overcultivation, and improper **irrigation.**

erosion   Process by which soil is carried away from a region by water or wind; can occur naturally or because of human activities, including deforestation, overgrazing, and various farming methods.

fertilizer   Chemical or natural substance used to boost the fertility of soil. Natural fertilizers consist of organic matter such as animal manure that add nutrients to the soil as well as **humus,** which improves soil's texture and ability to retain water and nutrients. Synthetic chemical fertilizers such as nitrate and phosphate compounds add nutrients but do not improve soil texture; they can also leach into underground water sources, potentially poisoning wildlife and humans.

groundwater   Water beneath the earth's surface that flows slowly between soil and rock and supplies wells and springs; held in underground reservoirs called **aquifers**.

hybridization   Cross-breeding of plants to combine the best traits of different species to produce crops more resistant to disease and with higher yields.

low-input agriculture   Farming that seeks to produce high yields using as few **fertilizers**, **pesticides**, and other material inputs as possible.

monoculture   Planting large areas of land with just one crop; often contributes to degradation because it does not restore nutrients to the soil.

organic farming   Cultivation using natural, organic fertilizers and natural pest control methods instead of chemical fertilizers and pesticides.

pesticides   Poisonous chemicals used to eliminate animal pests and weeds from crops; herbicides kill plants whereas insecticides kill insects and other pests.

salinization   Buildup of salt in soil, often exacerbated by irrigation; high salt concentrations can be toxic to plants.

swidden agriculture   Creating temporary agricultural plots by cutting back and burning off vegetative cover; also known as slash-and-burn farming.

terracing   Cutting slopes into level shelves to stop hillside erosion, increase surface area for planting, and retain rainwater.

waterlogging   The saturation of soil with irrigation water, which causes groundwater to rise to the surface, drowning plant roots.

INDEX

Deciduous forests, 77
Deforestation
    and agriculture, 66–68
    and climatic change, 72–75
    in nontropical forests, 75–77
    and species extinction, 68–72
Desalinization plants, 47
Desertification
    and agriculture, 88–89
    and livestock, 86–87, 88,
        91–95
    and population, 84–85, 90–91
Drainage systems, 45–46, 48
Drip irrigation, 47, 48
Dust Bowl, 55, 58

Ecuador, 101
Egypt, 40, 51, 52
Ehrlich, Paul, 85
Environmental Protection Agency,
    U.S. (EPA), 27
Erosion
    and agriculture, 53–58, 61–62
    natural function, 51–52
    and rivers, 59–60
    and termites, 62–63
Europe, 27, 58
Eutrophication, 27

Fertilizers, 24, 26–28, 34, 35, 37,
    43, 58
Food chain, 29

Global warming, 74, 97
Grameen Bank, 100–101
Grand Canyon, 51
Great Britain, 27, 36
Great Plains, 56, 92

Green algae, 27
Greenhouse effect, 74, 75
Greenhouse gases, 72, 73, 74, 75
Green Revolution, 25, 58
Guatemala, 79
Gullies, 55

Harvard University, 17, 68
Hedgerows, 62
Herbicides, 28
Himalayan watershed, 66
Huang He. *See* Yellow River
Humus, 14, 27
Hybrid crops, 24
Hydrological vacuum, 42

Iguanas, 79–81
India, 40, 42, 53, 66, 99
Indian Himalayas, 99
Indus River, 40
Indus River valley, 40, 42
Industrial farms, 36
Insecticides, 28
Integrated Pest Management (IPM),
    35
Intercropping, 36
Israel, 48, 49
Ivory Coast, 101

Japan, 27

Kansas, 58, 84
Kitching, Roger, 71

Land degradation. *See specific
    issues*
Las Vegas, Nevada, 40
Lateritic soil, 66

P I C T U R E   C R E D I T S

AP/Wide World Photos: pp. 53, 67, 75; The Bettmann Archive: pp. 25, 54; Buddy Mays Travel Stock: pp. 12, 62, 70, 85, 94; Bureau of Reclamation: p. 23; J. C. Dahilig/Bureau of Reclamation: pp. 38, 48; Mel Davis/Bureau of Reclamation: p. 44; Reuters/Bettmann Archive: p. 89; Gary Tong: pp. 16, 45, 86–87; Dean Tvedt/Wisconsin Department of Natural Resources: p. 28; UN Photo 148503/John Isaac: p. 100; UN Photo 150108/Carolyn Redenius: p. 64; UN Photo 150651/Philip Teuscher: p. 90; United Nations/Photo by B. P. Wolff: p. 96; United States Department of Agriculture: pp. 19, 31, 36; UPI/Bettmann Archive: pp. 41, 50, 57, 73, 76, 80, 82, 99; D. J. Voros/United States Fish and Wildlife Service: p. 30; Glade Walker/Bureau of Reclamation: p. 20; D. J. Weir/Bureau of Reclamation: p. 33; Wisconsin Department of Natural Resources: p. 78

ABOUT THE AUTHOR

MARK CHERRINGTON is the editor of *Earthwatch* magazine, published by the nonprofit scientific field organization of the same name. Through *Earthwatch* he has participated in half a dozen expeditions dealing with endangered wildlife, cultural survival, geology, limnology, and other subjects. He also spent a number of years as a professional musician. Cherrington received his master's degree in journalism from Boston University in 1985.

ABOUT THE EDITOR

RUSSELL E. TRAIN, currently chairman of the board of directors of the World Wildlife Fund and The Conservation Foundation, has had a long and distinguished career of government service under three presidents. In 1957 President Eisenhower appointed him a judge of the United States Tax Court. He served Lyndon Johnson on the National Water Commission. Under Richard Nixon he became under secretary of the Interior and, in 1970, first chairman of the Council on Environmental Quality. From 1973 to 1977 he served as administrator of the Environmental Protection Agency. Train is also a trustee or director of the African Wildlife Foundation; the Alliance to Save Energy; the American Conservation Association; Citizens for Ocean Law; Clean Sites, Inc.; the Elizabeth Haub Foundation; the King Mahendra Trust for Nature Conservation (Nepal); Resources for the Future; the Rockefeller Brothers Fund; the Scientists' Institute for Public Information; the World Resources Institute; and Union Carbide and Applied Energy Services, Inc. Train is a graduate of Princeton and Columbia Universities, a veteran of World War II, and currently resides in the District of Columbia.